TRANSFORMATIONS

Transforming
Vestries

CHURCH
PUBLISHING
INCORPORATED

JAMES LEMLER, SERIES EDITOR

Unless otherwise noted, the Scripture quotations contained herein are from the New Revised Standard Version Bible, copyright © 1989 by the Division of Christian Education of the National Council of Churches of Christ in the U.S.A. Used by permission. All rights reserved.

Scriptures marked KJV are taken from the KING JAMES VERSION (KJV): KING JAMES VERSION, public domain.

Scriptures marked *The Message* are taken from the THE MESSAGE: THE BIBLE IN CONTEMPORARY ENGLISH (TM): Scripture taken from THE MESSAGE: THE BIBLE IN CONTEMPORARY ENGLISH, copyright©1993, 1994, 1995, 1996, 2000, 2001, 2002. Used by permission of NavPress Publishing Group.

This book compiles text from the following sources, all published by Church Publishing: Katherine Tyler Scott, *Transforming Leadership* (2010); David Gortner, *Transforming Evangelism* (2008); Linda L. Grenz, *Transforming Disciples* (2008); James Lemler, *Transforming Congregations* (2008); C. K. Robertson, *Transforming Stewardship* (2009)

Church Publishing
19 East 34th Street
New York, NY 10016
www.churchpublishing.org

Cover design by Jennifer Kopec, 2Pug Design
Typeset by Denise Hoff

Library of Congress Cataloging-in-Publication Data

Title: Transforming vestries.
Description: New York, NY : Church Publishing, [2019] | Series: Transformations : the Episcopal Church in the 21st century | Includes bibliographical references and index.
Identifiers: LCCN 2018057979 (print) | LCCN 2019001556 (ebook) | ISBN 9781640652330 (ebook) | ISBN 9781640652323 (pbk. : alk. paper) | ISBN 9781640652330 (ebk.)
Subjects: LCSH: Episcopal Church--Government.
Classification: LCC BX5950 (ebook) | LCC BX5950 .T73 2019 (print) | DDC 254/.0373--dc23
LC record available at https://lccn.loc.gov/2018057979

Contents

A Note
from the Publisher

This series emerged as a partnership between the Office of Mission of the Episcopal Church and Church Publishing Incorporated, as a contribution to the mission of the church in a new century. We would like to thank James Lemler, series editor, for bringing the initial idea to us and for facilitating the series. We also want to express our gratitude to the Office of Mission for two partnership grants: the first brought all the series authors together for two creative days of brainstorming and fellowship; and the second is helping to further publicize the books of the series to the clergy and lay people of the Episcopal Church.

Series Preface

"Be ye transformed" (KJV). "Be transformed by the renewing of your minds" (NRSV). "Fix your attention on God. You'll be changed from the inside out" (*The Message*). Thus St. Paul exhorted the earliest Christian community in his writing to the Romans two millennia ago. This exhortation was important for the early church and it is urgent for the Episcopal Church to heed as it enters the twenty-first century. Be transformed. Be changed from the inside out.

Perhaps no term fits the work and circumstances of the church in the twenty-first century better than "transformation." We are increasingly aware of the need for change as we become ever more mission-focused in the life of the church, both internationally and domestically. But society as a whole is rapidly moving in new directions, and mission cannot be embraced in an unexamined way, relying on old cultural and ecclesiastical stereotypes and assumptions.

This new series, *Transformations: The Episcopal Church in the 21st Century,* addresses these issues in realistic and hopeful ways. Each book focuses on one area within the Episcopal Church that is urgently in need of transformation in order for the church to be effective in the twenty-first century: vocation, evangelism, preaching, congregational life, getting to know the Bible, leadership, Christian formation, worship, and stewardship. Each volume explains why a changed vision is essential, gives robust theological and biblical foundations, offers guidelines to best practices and positive trends, describes the necessary tools for change, and imagines how transformation will look.

Most Episcopalians will readily admit to not knowing the Bible and are reluctant to engage the Scriptures in a disciplined and regular way. We often hear the Bible only on Sundays, and even then it is heard in the context of the liturgy—through the words of the Book of Common Prayer and Hymnal—and interpreted through sermons.

Like Christians in the early church, today we live in a secular culture that can be apathetic and even hostile to Christianity. Living in a setting where people are not familiar with the message or narrative of Christian believing requires new responses and new kinds of mission for the Body of Christ. We believe this is a hopeful time for spiritual seekers and inquirers in the church. The gospel itself is fresh for this century. God's love is vibrant and real; God's mission can transform people's hopes and lives. Will we participate in the transformation? Will we be bearers and agents of transformation for others? Will we ourselves be transformed? This is the call and these are the urgent questions for the Episcopal Church in the twenty-first century.

But first, seek to be transformed. Fix your attention on God. You'll be changed from the inside out.

James B. Lemler, series editor

Acknowledgments

James Lemler and his visionary colleagues began the work of this series more than a decade ago. As I've worked to create this new volume, *Transforming Vestries,* by pulling material from existing books in the series, I've been delighted by their passion—and their accuracy (although I did pull a couple of references to the Yellow Pages).

As the Episcopal Church moves further into the twenty-first century, ignited by the mandates of the Jesus Movement for creation care, evangelism, and racial reconciliation and following the Way of Love, Church Publishing is pleased to offer this new resource. Designed primarily for vestries, the book is suitable for leaders of all sorts—those elected to the special ministry of vestry membership and those who lead from their location in the pew.

Church Publishing is grateful to all those who have written for this series, but acknowledges especially the authors whose work forms this book: James Lemler, Linda L. Grenz, David Gortner, C. K. Robertson, and Katherine Tyler Scott.

Chapter 1 first appeared in a more fulsome form as two chapters in *Transforming Leadership:* "The Call—Leadership as Vocation" and "The Sacramental Nature of Leadership." Chapter 2 has been edited from a chapter with the same name in *Transforming Evangelism*. Chapter 3 has been taken from *Transforming Disciples*, Chapter 4 from *Transforming Congregations*, and Chapter 5 first appeared as "'Suggested Route" in *Transforming Stewardship*.

Nancy Bryan, *volume editor*

chapter 1

Leadership as Sacramental Vocation

Katherine Tyler Scott

When a culture loses its authorized version, the body politic fragments, and its spiritual prosperity withers.

—Bruno Bettelheim

Although differences in polity and theology across the Anglican Communion seem irreconcilable at times, what I find constructive in this time of turmoil is that the current conflicts have precipitated a period of reexamination of identity and purpose. The church has been motivated, and in a few instances pushed, to identify what its beliefs are at the core and to create a common understanding from which to engage and reorder relationships with others in the Communion.

The Search for Coherence, the monograph based on the research by William Sachs following the 2003 General Convention of the Episcopal Church, describes the church as being in a state of "creative incoherence." This is the result of old ways no longer working and a lack of the conviction and courage necessary to risk changing. The ensuing modern-day Tower of Babel reveals one of the challenges of being on the margin, of being in between the familiar and the yet-unborn, that of having vocational amnesia. The state of creative incoherence beckons us to return to our foundational sense of who we are and why we exist. It is a call to the vocation so movingly articulated in the Baptismal Covenant.

The Baptismal Covenant conveys our Christian call; it is the contractual agreement addressing the universal questions of identity, our relationship to God, and our obligations to one another. In the reading of, listening to, and practicing of this sacred covenant we enter into the heart of God, a God who promises us community and connection, who holds and cradles us, a God who provides the peace and belonging we crave. We come to know an expectant God who asks us to fulfill our obligations to seek and serve Christ in all persons, to treat them with dignity and respect, and to persevere in resisting evil. When we are sent into the world "in peace, to love and serve the Lord," we are being sent out to live this covenant in some of the most challenging conditions. When asked whether we will seek to meet God's expectations in the covenant, we respond, "We will, with God's help." In this response we are expressing our strong desire to live out our baptismal promises, while knowing that we cannot enter into the gap between reality and the ideal without the help of the Divine.

The Baptismal Covenant calls us all to a common endeavor, and yet unless the deeper meaning of these words is translated into practical day-to-day actions, they lose their power to transform. The loss of meaning results in a state of creative incoherence—a state of hollow ritual and busyness lacking meaning. The church continues to clarify how the ministry of all the baptized should manifest itself. The working out of these shifting roles and relationships is vital in obtaining a creative, coherent state of leadership in the church.

Implicit in the Baptismal Covenant is a template for the relationship and responsibilities of laity and clergy. It evokes shared leadership and mutual ministry that, when faithfully practiced, reinvigorates the church and expands its mission and impact across the globe. The Baptismal Covenant sees leadership in everyone and at every level. It claims a new paradigm of leadership, the DNA of which is embodied in the covenant.

When the Israelites wailed in the desert, "What is to become of us?" they had forgotten who and whose they were and what they were called to do. The Israelites had lost the signposts that helped them to remember their identity and ultimate destiny, the guides that had provided them with security and direction. Likewise, the church is experiencing a passage of confusion and loss, and in our contemporary desert time the question of what is to become of us still hangs in the air. The story of Exodus reminds us that in the in-between times, historical amnesia and loss of identity is a recipe for prolonged suffering.

We are being called to have the faith and courage to move with grace-filled patience and trust, knowing that we will arrive at the Promised Land with God's help. Remembering our vocation, living out our Baptismal Covenant, will help us to endure and triumph.

The transformation of the church can be accomplished without losing what is precious to it, but it cannot avert change. Whether it is accepting a revised Book of Common Prayer or the service leaflet in its place, the loss of an esteemed lay or clergy leader or the departure of parishes and splitting or consolidation of dioceses, a period of grief and disorientation will ensue. Any time our understanding of identity, authority, and vocation is called into question, the real work is to live into and through the dissonance that automatically comes with change, emerging with an even stronger faith.

This is work that cannot be done alone; learning to do the work of transformation requires a community of faithful learners and leaders. The church should be the primary institution preparing leaders for this work. If it accepts this vocation the church will enter a "renaissance of mission" that will revitalize the church and plant the seeds of transformation in the world.

We will need a set of skills and resources designed to bring about such transformation. The resources described on the following pages will enable leaders to read differing historical and cultural realities deftly, to develop competence in group dynamics and development, and to gain expertise in facilitating adaptive work. Additional skills in managing change and resolving conflict, translating facts into a meaningful narrative, creating communities of learning, engendering cultures of trust, and manifesting courage, integrity, and authenticity will be essential.

Understanding Organizational Culture

In addition to the larger societal, global, and historical contexts in which your parish sits, obtaining a broader and deeper understanding and knowledge of organizational culture is critical to the work of transformation. Culture is a complex concept, and its creation and ongoing development is one of the key responsibilities of the new leadership. The ability to read culture and to manage the complexity of human and organizational experiences and perspectives that exist within it is the sine qua non of leadership.

Terry Deal, coauthor of *Corporate Cultures* and an expert observer of systems, describes culture as "the way we do things around here." This pithy aphorism captures the behavioral aspects of culture, without highlighting the deeper underlying structures and unconscious assumptions that frequently evolve into unquestioned beliefs and unexamined behaviors. Both aspects of culture compose a hologram through which we can view how a parish perceives, believes, and thinks about itself, how it is perceived by the larger public, and the impact of these perceptions on mission. The following typology might assist in exploring the depth and breadth of culture that the most effective leaders learn to master. The levels indicate the degree of visibility.

A TOOL FOR READING ORGANIZATIONAL CULTURE

	LEVELS	FOCUS	LEADERSHIP ROLE
EXTERNAL	ARTIFACTUAL	Literature, image, attire, rituals, public materials	Public face of the organization's mission and message; myth maker
EXTERNAL	STRUCTURAL	Organization, structure, distribution of resources, space utilization, markets, production	Enabler of competence, manager, administrator
INTERNAL	BEHAVIORAL	Management of people, trust, relationships, communication	Creator of community, skill-builder, educator
INTERNAL	PHILOSOPHICAL	Management of values, beliefs, vocation, mission, philanthropic interests, community	Creator of culture, storyteller, connector of ideas and actions, interpreter, translator
INTERNAL	FOUNDATIONAL	Basic assumptions about existence, purposes, relationship to larger world, spirituality	Meaning-maker, creator of spiritual model for authenticity and integrity, integration, groundedness

The Artifactual Level of Culture

The artifactual level showcases the obvious and visible aspects of culture most easily associated with an organization. For a church these include the physical location, architecture, worship space, placement of the altar, furnishings, and art, as well as tangible aspects of church life such as the service bulletins, website, nametags, bulletin boards, and newsletters. We can gain some understanding of a parish culture through observing such phenomena.

At this level of culture, status and authority are equated with formal position, title, and institutional name. The leader can easily become the personification of the parish and the bearer of its institutional myth. The identity of the leader and that of the parish can merge into a blended image of projections from past experiences and unspoken expectations of parish members. Differentiating between projection and reality is important in the work of transformational leadership. Differentiation means that the leader will be able to clearly know the difference between who they are and whom others believe them to be. One of the hallmarks of transformational leadership is the ability to differentiate self from institutional *persona* while still accepting the role of institutional narrator, a responsibility that paradoxically requires more than the ability to tell the institution's story; it involves knowing and telling the leader's own story. The *deeper* knowledge of self prevents the seduction of a leader to believe automatically either the accolades or criticisms.

The Structural and Behavioral Levels of Culture

Both the structural and behavioral levels of culture unearth tangible forms of the organization of people and worship and how congregants participate in ministry inside the parish and out in the world. The weekly and annual calendars of parish activities, the worship bulletins, and an organizational chart are all indicators of how the leadership and life of a parish are ordered. If these artifacts do not exist, this is also important information about parish culture.

Vestry and committee meetings are other venues that help a leader to decipher communication dynamics and patterns, mission, and the distribution and exercise of power. Questions that can be asked of such gatherings include:

- How are members oriented? Prepared to lead?
- Who convenes the meeting?
- Who attends?
- Who plans the agenda?
- How often and where do they meet?
- When and how do the meetings begin?
- How is leadership experienced?
- What opportunities are there for Bible study and/or theological reflection?
- What frameworks and norms exist for discussion and decision-making?
- How is mission integrated?

The answers to questions such as these are revealing of the culture of a parish.

Another way to access the various levels of culture is to attend the ubiquitous coffee hour following a parish worship service, and consider the following questions:

- How do people hear about it?
- Where is it located? How accessible is it?
- What time is it scheduled?
- Who attends?
- What are people given to eat and drink?
- Do the clergy attend? With whom do they talk?
- Are name tags available, and are they worn?
- How are visitors greeted, and then treated?
- How are members treated?

When my husband and I first moved to the diocese of Indianapolis, we visited every parish in the deanery searching for a home. One Sunday we visited a parish that to our surprise had the bishop visiting them. When we walked into the church, no one looked at or greeted us. We found our seats and sat in observant silence. We were barely greeted during the Peace and, after a beautiful service, we processed out to attend the reception. Members joyfully greeted one another and gathered in clusters of familiar friends. The bishop spotted us and came over to hug us. His huge smile and embrace of us was food for our souls and a gesture of our friendship. No one in this congregation knew he was a friend of ours until that moment. After this, a number of people came up to say hello and to welcome us. As we left to go home, we looked at each other and knew that we would not return to this parish. The structural elements of the culture were exactly what we expected—everything was identifiably Episcopalian—but the behavior of the congregants was the antithesis of an inclusive, hospitable, loving community. We immediately learned that in this parish status mattered more than the Baptismal Covenant.

These levels of culture require leadership with excellent organizational and planning skills. They need leaders with strong administrative skills and the ability to match people and resources in ways that maximize the parish's ability to accomplish its mission. Even when there is staff designated to do this work, the rector must be capable of supervising the work. The clergy leader is responsible for the workings of the whole system and its parts and serves as the "creator of community." Creating an environment in which people feel purpose, belonging, a shared identity, security, and trust is a responsibility that sets the transforming leader apart from others.

An example of this kind of leadership can be seen in a healthy and growing parish that is part of a diocese experiencing budgetary problems and chronic leadership lethargy. The rector recognized the need to attract younger individuals and families and began by first educating the vestry about the need to do this. Although this highly successful congregation seemed an unlikely candidate for major change, this rector was able to show the congregation its future through a study of demographics in the Episcopal Church. He engaged the vestry in analyzing the research data and its implications for the parish. Once the vestry members understood the urgency, and realized that the initiative was not about "fixing a failure" but about ensuring the future, they supported the change and the hiring of a staff person to develop programs and services for this demographic.

The message was clear: "We are serious about our ministry to young individuals and families." The parish is seeing a revitalization of youth programs, and more activities for young parents and children are planned. This particular leader framed this initiative in ways that helped all of the parish feel included in this process of forming a culture of life-long learning so that everyone, from cradle to maturity, could see that their formation is always important, even as more resources and attention were being provided to a younger demographic.

The Philosophical Level of Culture

The fourth level of culture is not so easily or directly ascertained as that of the structural and behavioral levels. This is the place of unquestioned assumptions and unchallenged core beliefs and values. Most of the behaviors at the philosophical level are unconscious, yet they have an enormous effect on the community of a parish. This level is deeper than what we can see, and it goes to the heart of *why* a congregation gathers to worship. It is where the meaning of the more visible and outward signs of life in a faith community exists.

An example of this level is the way in which a congregation "passes the Peace." This act reveals deeply held values and beliefs about the ecclesial responsibility for creating relationships and a community of belonging. It is a manifestation of a congregation's beliefs about physical touch and connection, the role of worship, the importance of community, and the meaning of the Eucharist. During the passing of the Peace in one parish, nearly all of the people move fluidly across and up and down the aisles, erupting into quiet but brief exchanges, hugging, smiling, and greeting warmly all whom they encounter. In another parish the parishioners pass the Peace only to those who are in their immediate proximity. In still another congregation a number of people remain kneeling in prayer during the passing of the Peace. These practices reflect the cultural differences that lie at the deeper levels of parish life.

An examination of why a parish engages in certain practices is a way to ensure that there will not be a disconnect between the activities of a parish and the beliefs they espouse as precious or unchanging. Without congruence between their values and actions, parishes can lose a sense of integrity and can easily become overextended and frenzied in their program offerings. Actions and activities that are not tethered to core values can easily lead to forms of institutional narcissism, meaningless group activity, and mission silos. They may possess the trappings of community but lack the substance and meaning of what makes a community.

The Foundational Level of Culture

The last level of culture is what I call the foundational level, and is very close to the philosophical level, but it is even less visible. Core values and faith identity reside here; this is the level of spiritual depth in which something greater and more powerful than anyone or anything is encountered. This level houses the basic assumptions about why we exist, our purpose and reason for being, and our relationship to the Divine. It is the place of connection to a larger reality and a transcendent circle of belonging, a place of deep knowing in which we understand and feel that we are all part of the same Divine Source of all life.

This deeply spiritual and transcendent place has no easy or direct route to it. It can't be commanded or demanded to appear but is most accessible through attention to the other levels of culture and through a disciplined practice of reflection, prayer, meditation, and the study of Scripture.

Many of us have experienced the gift of grace and congruence in which we feel connected to the Divine. I recall a beautiful homily at the ordination of a priest that left the congregation breathless and in awe, or the experience of my parish when our building was undergoing renovation and we were invited to worship on a glorious Easter Sunday in a Jewish synagogue. The ability to cross such divides and be in relationship and unity with those whom we may usually see as only different was a taste of the transcendent, of what heaven is. These experiences not only leave us speechless, but inspired and full of hope that we might be able to live out God's love after all.

We have also likely experienced times when actions are not synchronous with what is said or believed:

- a parish perceives itself as warm and friendly but does not greet newcomers at coffee hour;
- church members express discomfort when a homeless, disheveled person wanders into the Sunday service;
- volunteers are not given adequate meeting space or the resources necessary to carry out an assignment;
- lay leaders are engaged in diocesan and national mission but are offered no parish support;
- members serve in positions of responsibility indefinitely without being given an honorable out;
- lay employees are offered pay and benefits that are close to or below the poverty level.

If disconnects such as these are not recognized and resolved over time, the incongruence between actions and the foundational beliefs and values deepens and widens, leaving a groove of undifferentiated and chronic dis-ease, a pernicious form of cynicism, and a significant erosion of trust in the authenticity of the clergy and the congregation.

In one urban parish with which we worked, there was a large network of guilds and ad hoc program groups, each with its own distinctive history, agenda, and fundraising activities. Each group felt it was contributing to the mission of the parish and serving legitimate needs. There was poor communication and little or no collaboration between them. The larger purpose of the church and its mission of unity in Christ had become buried in a thicket of competitive activities and endless meetings.

Understandably, the newly called rector wanted to disband these traditional and often competitive groups. He felt they were "a drag on the mission," even though there appeared to be a strong allegiance to them in the parish. Our counsel was to start with first understanding the history and the existence of guilds as a way to obtain valuable data about the culture. The rector and the vestry could then better determine what should be retained and what should not.

The rector visited the guilds and groups, observed their activities, talked with the members, and learned a lot about them and the parish itself. Because he took the time to understand the history and more accurately read the culture, he was able to understand how the guilds and groups had come into being, how they had veered away from the larger purpose, and how they had become disconnected from the deeper roots of the parish's mission.

The adaptive work of this rector was to realign the beliefs and actions. He invited the groups' leaders to weekly Bible study and created opportunities to bring them together on projects that served the whole parish. He also started a new group for professional working women that met in the evenings rather than during the day. This opened up the membership, and the groups began to become less resistant to change. In doing so, they began to collaborate, and eliminated the duplication of projects and constant fundraising efforts.

Fredrica Harris Thompsett's observation in *We Are Theologians* bears repeating here: "With so much going on in our society and world, *what* we choose to notice reveals *who* we are." Traditionally, Episcopalians are called to understand a wider reality and be able to fully engage in a panoply of differing opinions and positions. This practiced discipline means that our leaders must have the capacity to hold the "tension of the opposites" together. They are to help the congregation pay attention to what is relevant and essential, and to remember that what is paid attention to affects identity and calling. Can the church minister to the world with authenticity and integrity when it denies these tensions and refuses to contribute to understanding?

The church is being called to pay attention to the current state of "creative incoherence" that William Sachs discovered in his research. The mind-numbing busyness in some parishes and the beautiful trappings and symbols that are treasured in others will not in the long run be a substitute for the search for answers to the ancient, universal, and profound vocational and mission questions we all experience: Who are we? For what purpose do we exist? What are we called to do? They are profoundly and deeply religious in nature. Those in positions of leadership in the church are charged with the primary responsibility to create opportunity and spaces in which to wrestle with these questions.

A Tool for Understanding Philanthropy

Every parish includes some form of outreach in its definition of identity and mission, but these efforts can become imprisoned in unquestioned assumptions and unexamined mission activities. Understanding the different traditions of philanthropy and making a conscious decision about which one the parish must practice is a first step in making what is implicit explicit. A schema developed by D. Susan Wisely, former director of evaluation at the Lilly Endowment, defines three major philanthropic traditions: charity, improvement, and social reform.

Transforming leaders examine the foundational level of parish culture to determine which tradition is embedded and influences practices in the parish. For example, if charity is the tradition of giving in a parish, the primary intent is to alleviate suffering. The compassion for someone in immediate need recognizes the state of crisis and guides the desire to give *now*. If the tradition is improvement of the lives of those in need, then the strategy changes to one of equipping the individual or group with the capacity to improve their lives through education and opportunities. The initiative can begin in the now, but it will take time for change to happen. The third tradition of giving is social reform, the intent to change the system that creates and perpetuates the problem. In this instance, the primary strategy is a long-term effort requiring focused investment of time, money, and people resources.

Each of these strategies has an impact, but not all of them will be transformative in nature. Each one progressively requires more of the involvement of the donor; each one requires increasing levels of adaptive skills, those skills required when the problem is complex and unclear and the leader must engage those with the problem in resolving it. The questions with which parish leaders will need to wrestle include:

- What are our guiding principles?
- What are the implicit assumptions in our actions?
- What is our mission and vocation?

- What is the ultimate impact that we want our giving to have?
- Who is it that we are intending to serve?
- Are our actions congruent with our values?

These classifications of philanthropic practice provide a framework within which parishes can address these questions, evaluate their philosophy and mission of giving, and determine the desired impact. This is a responsible way the church can determine if it is engaged in transformational work and whether it has the right leadership in place to accomplish it.

Leadership is the fundamental process by which culture is formed and transformed, and the leader is the chief architect of culture. This means also having an understanding of the dynamics of change and how to manage it. Transformational leadership requires an understanding of how individuals, organizations, and communities respond to change.

Leading Change

The gap between ending the current reality and moving others into a future that looks different is the most challenging task for a leader who desires transformation. We know that the leader of transformational change must know the institutional story, the organization's historical trajectory over time, and the mega-narrative in which the organization's capacity for managing change resides. This capacity emerges from the key changes the organization has experienced, how it responded to these changes, and what organizational learning occurred as a result. Determining the parish's ability to manage change reveals the strengths upon which to build as well as the weaknesses.

The most effective leaders of change are not only historians; they are analysts and prophets too. Once they understand the past and have read the larger reality in which they live, they can use their assessment to find the best way to proceed to the preferred future. This plan needs to be inspired by vision and translated into a blueprint for change that clearly explicates the urgency for change, the purpose and goals, and the strategies for achieving success. A thorough assessment and analysis can also reveal the degree of change being proposed and how to anticipate and deal with the ways the changes will affect particular individuals or groups of people.

The leader of transformational change is aware of both the type of change induced and level of culture that will be most affected. This awareness will help determine the most effective strategies for launching and managing successful change. The leader's assessment of the organization's capacity, readiness, and skill level is essential. It may be prudent to begin with lower risk, technical, or structural interventions as preparation for more transformative change if the congregation has had little experience with managing change successfully.

The deeper levels of organizational culture demand a higher level of skills. Clergy are not omnipotent, and expecting them to do and be everything is a setup for failure. Acknowledging their limitations and their gifts can liberate them to learn to appreciate and use the gifts and skills already present in the parish community. Acknowledging both gifts and limitations reduces a leader's blind spot and provides a broader, more comprehensive picture of what the leadership in the parish needs in order to bring about transformational change.

Responses to the Change Process

Change is a constant reality and managing and leading it is a huge challenge for leaders. Change at any level of culture stresses an organization. The degree of stress is dependent on the degree of change, and if change stirs up questions about identity and mission, then the leader has to understand the psychological effects precipitated by change.

ORGANIZATIONAL RESPONSES TO CHANGE

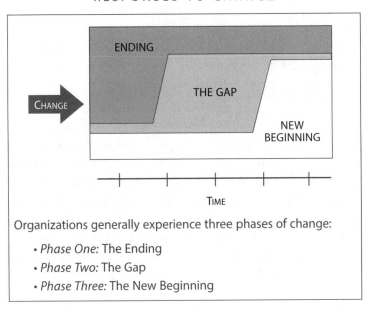

Organizations generally experience three phases of change:

- *Phase One:* The Ending
- *Phase Two:* The Gap
- *Phase Three:* The New Beginning

Whenever major change in a congregation is introduced, this transition process begins, unleashing many psychological states within individuals in the parish. For leaders who are managing and leading change, it is imperative to understand what these are.

Phase One: The Ending

The introduction of change is felt as an ending by the majority of people. Nearly 75 percent of them will be in a state of denial and resistance. About 10 percent will have already moved into Phase Two, and the remainder will be in Phase Three. The leader of change is what I call a Phase Three Leader, trying to influence those who are opposed to change. If such leaders do not understand this gap, their actions may end up reinforcing the Phase One emotions.

Phase Two: The Gap

In this phase change is experienced as a time of ambiguity, anxiety, and confusion. A variety of emotions are experienced in this phase, from hating the change to already living it. In any given parish experiencing major transition, over time more people will move into this phase, as fewer people remain in the earlier phase of denial and resistance.

Phase Three: The New Beginning

In Phase Three about 75 percent of the congregants have embraced the new beginning, while about 10 percent remain in the Gap and 10 percent remain in denial and resistance. If everything has been done to bring people along toward the new vision, the challenge for a leader in this phase is to focus on those who have embraced the change. This is the big "if," because coercing or cheerleading change will not work in the first two phases. People are in shock and grief, and their emotions and the level of anxiety make it difficult to be persuaded by reasoned logic.

The leader's task in bringing about transformation is to help people let go. Leadership and change consultant William Bridges says that most change initiatives fail because the work of letting go is ignored. Rushing people through the phases only contributes to regression and a weakened commitment to the desired change.

Managing the Change Process

An inability to assess and analyze the culture completely and accurately can lead to an intervention that communicates an unintended message to an organization. This happened in one parish when the priest-in-charge hired a strategic planner with considerable background in corporate planning but with no knowledge of or experience with the Episcopal Church. The intended message of the importance of a disciplined approach to planning for mission became blurred and bogged down in a confusing parade of exercises and incomprehensible reports devoid of the spirit and grace needed to revitalize this congregation.

Matching an intervention to a particular level of culture and phase of change is important. If this is not done, it can look as though the leader is impervious to the true needs of followers and lay leaders. In one corporate-sized parish the members of the altar guild always met briefly with the priest for prayer just before the service; after the service the priest would hand his vestments to them and warmly thank them for their service. This ritual, developed over the years, was more than a pastoral expression of gratitude; to the guild members it was an affirmation of their ministry, and it had come to have significant meaning. When a new priest arrived, he decided it was more efficient to vest and disrobe in his office. He did not talk with the guild members, so he was unaware of their practice and its meaning. When several members of the guild gathered enough courage to talk with the priest about this change, he perceived their efforts as an attempt to control him. He held his ground, and in the process destroyed something precious in that community and in the relationship between the priest and the lay leaders: the recognition and affirmation of vocation. The priest's ignorance of the parish tradition, along with the historical mythology of powerful altar guilds he brought with him, made it impossible for him to see the spiritual significance of this practice. This leader missed an opportunity to learn the deeper level of meaning in this church's subculture. On the surface, the change seemed inconsequential, but this misunderstanding of the intent and impact of a particular tradition created a rift between the priest and those in the altar guild.

Whatever the level at which change is introduced, the leader's task is to ensure that as much alignment and congruence as possible exists between the types of change and the levels of culture. This engenders trust in leadership, and enables those who are being asked to change to leave their comfort zones and take the necessary risks to achieve personal and organizational transformation.

The Sacramental Nature of Leadership

The clarion call for church leadership is occurring at a time of enormous societal change. We are witnessing any number of shifting realities:

- an ever-widening gap between the poor and the wealthy;
- a persistent hostility toward difference;
- a slow, steady decline of relationship networks that form the foundation for community cohesion and problem-solving;
- a loss of shared identity and belonging;
- a rise in individualism and insularity;
- a decrease in the public's trust in leaders and institutions;
- a continuing retreat into privatization of public services;
- economic volatility, the rising costs of health care, pervasive poverty, and increased competition for resources.

In addition to these changes, the historic divides of race, class, and gender continue in varying degrees, making the litany of problems and grim statistics sobering.

What is it that strengthens those leaders who choose not to retreat from these changes, those who believe that they can make a meaningful difference in situations frequently filled with anxiety and stress? Why do they continue to support struggling outreach programs? What gives them the sense that they can overcome intolerance and prejudice and open up communities walled off by privilege and ignorance? What is it that makes them continue to reach out to change abject conditions and refuse to surrender to adversity? More than any one thing, I believe it is the capacity to see their leadership as spiritually based—indeed, as *sacramental*.

It is difficult to live the words of Paul to the church in Rome, and the church finds it even more difficult to manifest the belief that we are indeed "one body in Christ, and individually members one of another" in times of complex change and uncertainty. We must remember, however, that the history and shape of community has always been influenced by religious values and beliefs. It is through religious institutions and leaders that Americans give expression to the belief that we have a shared responsibility for one another. Much of our voluntary service is motivated by religious belief and civic responsibility. Inherent in community service and philanthropy is the expectation that citizens in a democracy have a responsibility to be involved in identifying and addressing the concerns and issues of their communities and of the world.

The value Americans have placed on voluntary action for the public good was, and is, integral to an understanding of who we are as citizens and as Christians. In living out the historical legacy of caring for those less fortunate we experience the pull and tug between self-interest *and* the common good.

Alexis de Tocqueville, in *Democracy in America,* described our penchant for individualism as "a calm and considered feeling which disposes each citizen to isolate themselves from the masses and withdraw into a circle of family and friends; with this little society formed to their tastes, they gladly leave the greater society to look after itself." He also said that the danger of individualism was that it could lead to "being shut up in the solitude of our own hearts." The tension we experience is in the desire for autonomy and the reality of our interdependence. Leadership that is transformational recognizes this paradox-induced tension and strives to temper unfettered individualism and the tyranny of the majority. Transformational leadership accepts responsibility for holding these tensions and enables followers to manage the ambiguity and anxiety long enough to obtain a balanced perspective that avoids self-sacrifice or pious isolation.

Perhaps the most challenging work for church leaders in our time is confronting the hard lines drawn between our private and public lives that deplete both sectors of the full use of ourselves in service to mission. Dichotomies and divides between people persist and can threaten the emergence and sustainability of the kind of community Paul imagined. We are in danger of losing the meaning of an inclusive community; in too many instances we have retained the "habits" of community but have lost the "heart" of it. The loss of community parallels the demise of language that expresses our interdependence and our vision of unity. How can the church cultivate a deeper understanding of shared responsibility to hold others in trust—to care for those we may never know, in a time we will never see? How can we help reclaim the necessary habits and practices that flow from understanding that we are all "one body in Christ"?

In the work we have done with civic, philanthropic, business, and religious leaders, I have seen many whose deepest desire is to strengthen the core values, character, and commitment to service of their staff, members, and other constituents. Their desire is to improve the quality of life for all in their communities. But I believe it is the church that is the one institution whose vocation is to implant and nurture this desire. It is the church in which we learn about the mutual responsibility we have for one another, where we witness the strength of our connectedness, and where we learn how to keep our covenant to bring about unity. It is the church that is being called in this time to develop and nurture leaders with a sense of character, calling, congruence, and commitment— a matrix that strengthens mission.

These qualities help prevent us from being shut up in the solitude of our own hearts. They enable us to move from isolation and insularity into caring and meaningful service to others. It is the church that helps to shape the habits of the mind and practices of the heart that prepare us to fulfill the great commission to baptize all nations, to respond to Christ's command to greet the stranger, tend the sick, provide for the poor, and feed the hungry. It is the vocation of lay and clergy leaders to create the conditions in which followers can learn how to live out genuinely responsible, ethical, and spiritual lives.

Character, Calling, Congruence, and Commitment: A Matrix of Mission

A core belief that infuses policy and practice for many parishes where this sacramental view of leadership is held is that everything and everyone that God has created has the spark of God within. Leaders in these churches see their ministry as helping others discover this spark and live their passion: it is passion that drives the congregation. That passion might be understood as the energy or fuel that is essential for the car that is the parish to run. "Vision is like the steering wheel, providing the focus and direction needed to get to the destination."

Another essential element to the work of transformational leadership: teamwork. When passion is evoked it drives involvement. Ministry can naturally lead to silo-building unless everyone intentionally remains connected and understands the importance of working together. The question must continually be asked, "Where does God want to lead the church?" The answer resides in the collective sharing of God's wisdom with each other.

The "spark of God" is metaphorical, and the practices emanating from this image have led to an impressive transformation in the church and the community it serves. It is invigorating to contemplate what a culture is like when everyone in the congregation feels that within themselves is the "spark of God"—the manifestation of God's existence in human form. The leadership in such an environment is an outward expression of an inward presence of the Divine—leadership as sacrament.

What Is Sacramental Leadership?

According to the Catechism in the Book of Common Prayer, sacraments are "outward and visible signs of inward and spiritual grace." Leadership as sacrament embraces the skills and tasks of leading others as the embodiment and expression of faith. This kind of leadership is grounded in the knowledge that our very lives are a gift from God, a gift that came from the ultimate sacrifice, a gift to be shared with the world. The noted author on spirituality Tad Dunne writes, "Without faith, charity towards the neighbor washes away on the first rainy day. With faith, charity keeps surprising itself on how much self-sacrifice it is willing to endure and towards how many different people it is willing to pour out active, caring love."[1] Sacramental leadership pours out this active, caring love, rooted in a deep faith. It sees the congregation as the body of Christ, and all its actions as the *embodiment* of religious beliefs and core values expressed with congruence, authenticity, and integrity.

Sacramental leadership recognizes that we are all held in trust by a larger Love, transcendent of any particular clergy, lay leader, or congregation; a Love that connects all of us and that obligates us to care for one another. Leadership, seen and practiced as a sacrament, encourages this Love to flourish, creating and connecting a congregation that is in loving and faithful relationship with one another. The relationship between leaders and their followers is transformed because authority is shared, expectations and boundaries are clear, and mission and ministry are defined as including gifts from each order.

Leadership as sacrament integrates the different realms of our lives—the personal and the professional, the individual and the institutional, the private and the public, the subjective and the objective. It enables people to live out their lives "in whole cloth," to be fully who they are called to be—a spiritual practice in and of itself. A result is that our actions are more aligned with our words. Both shadow and light are acknowledged parts of the human condition, and their expression will not allow destructive energy to fester and grow.

The following are eight areas of practice that, if framed as a discipline of sacramental leadership, would be transformational.

---

1   Tad Dunne, *Lonergan and Spirituality: Towards a Spiritual Integration* (Chicago: Loyola University Press, 1985), 123.

The Sacramental Practice
of Strategic Planning

As most congregations know, planning for the future is simply good stewardship practice. Like any institution, churches must be fiscally responsible and exercise good fiduciary judgment, but unlike secular institutions, they must plan in service to a larger vision and vocation. Strategic planning can be an example of sacramental leadership. The decision to plan for the future is an act of faith, a statement of trust that in the coming together of human intent and Divine guidance we can influence the future and affect generations to come.

The sacramental practice of planning begins with historical reflection. Such reflection reveals the presence of the Divine in our lives and how it has been manifest in our lives and faith communities over time. Being aware of what and who has shaped us individually and corporately ingrains an awareness within us that as followers of Christ we are also followers of the cross—the ultimate symbol of transformation. Through the pain of death we will experience the joy of resurrection and we will be transformed; through suffering, we will be redeemed.

Sacramental leadership has the responsibility continually to tell the story of both the institutional church and Scripture, and to create and sustain a culture and community of calling and action that is grounded in that story. If as Frederick Buechner says, "God calls us to the place where our deep gladness and the world's deep hunger meet," a planning process can lead to an intersection of both the personal and corporate realms of our lives. The process needs to be infused with an openness to the unknown, a desire to serve God, and the knowledge that our beliefs are to be expressed in both word and deed. The sacramental leaders' approach to strategic planning begins with this theological grounding. What might the impact of the planning process be if it were to begin with Bible study? What if those responsible for the steward-ship of the future began with hearing and discussing the story of the rich man who stored and hoarded his resources? Might this lead to an in-depth discussion of how easily we can idolize what is perishable and forget what is permanent? How easy it is to be captured by the illusion of control and be driven by a sense of scarcity rather than abundance? Such an approach could help planning committees to see again how fleeting the existence of possessions is and how constant is the existence of God's abundant love and unfailing grace.

Whatever planning process a parish might use, it has to be tethered to a much broader and deeper understanding of how what it produces will be "outward and visible signs of inward and spiritual grace." When planning is a prac-tice of sacramental leadership, those involved will not be so obsessed with outcomes that they become more important than whether the process is one that creates a stronger, more cohesive, mission-based worshiping community, one that is well prepared to respond responsibly and ethically to the future. Such a process strengthens the faith and core values of a community. This approach does not preclude competent fund development, the establishment of reasonable financial goals, or the establishment of rigorous systems of account-ability. It emphasizes the significance of matching who we say we are with what we actually do. Rather than giving the illusion that we have total control over the future, it posi-tions congregations to see the fuller truth of their existence and to adapt to seismic change without losing the core of who they are. Whatever direction is decided, the parish and its leaders will be grounded in a knowledge of faith, and of their unique character and culture. Two examples of the sac-ramental practice of leadership follow.

The Sacramental Practice
of Letting Go

The rector of a twenty-year-old midwestern parish began to think about retirement several years before she would be canonically required to do so. She realized that her own planning process was intricately connected to the parish's need to begin strategic planning. Knowing that a conversation about this was imminent, she enlisted the assistance of a consultant, who helped her identify a group of congregational leaders to join with her in organizing and implementing the entire process. Each of the planning group's meetings began and ended with a moment of quiet reflection and prayer. The group agreed that the purpose of planning was to prepare for the transition in leadership and to ensure the health and vitality of the parish beyond the long tenure of the clergy leader.

The participation of all of the members in the congregation was sought through surveys, interviews, newsletters, and focus groups. Through this process, they identified major issues, concerns, and needs that needed to be addressed in the planning process. The planning group also canvassed leaders in the diocese and in their community, and pulled together a report of their findings for discussion and interpretation at a planning retreat.

At the retreat, a vast array of memorabilia—pictures, reports, and brochures that reflected past parish events—were displayed. Members signed in on the time line and recalled their reasons for coming to the parish. In the planning retreat they each described significant internal and external events that affected and shaped the parish over time. This process enabled members to remember what they were seeking when they first came to the parish. Many spoke of looking for a spiritual home and identified the qualities and characteristics of the parish that drew them in and helped them to stay.

The reflection on their history revealed the parish's uniqueness and its capacity to respond to change over time. More importantly, it solidified the members' commitment to mission and strengthened their desire to be a community of faith dedicated to the spiritual support of members and potential members. The group was able to differentiate between physical growth and spiritual growth. Both were deemed to be important—physical growth could create the space in which their worship takes place, while spiritual growth creates and sustains the caring, cohesive community of faith.

The planning group was able to face its anxieties about the loss of their long-term clergy leader. They drew on their faith in something greater than themselves and realized their dependence on each other would help them discern what God was calling them to do and to be. They had the courage to be patient and prudent in their deliberations and to be pastoral in a very sensitive situation.

Through understanding planning as an action of the sacramental nature of leadership, the planning process increased this congregation's commitment and desire to strengthen its ministry. The rector and the congregation could begin to let go of one another in a constructive, life-giving way. Because they saw planning as a practice of sacramental leadership, and not just a technical exercise, the parish could start to celebrate the current rector's tenure, accept the departure, and begin the work of becoming spiritually prepared to call the next leader without infecting the search with fear or reactionary responses.

The Sacramental Practice
of Speaking the Truth in Love

The second example of a church that engaged in a planning process led by leadership as a sacramental practice is an East Coast endowed parish. In 2003, this church found itself at the center of the post–General Convention controversy arising from the affirmation of the Diocese of New Hampshire's election of Gene Robinson, an openly gay bishop. In protest, six parishes in the diocese refused to send in their diocesan apportionments and also refused to have the bishop in the diocese confirm their youth.

The rector of this congregation, which was experiencing some of the tension and turmoil that other parishes were manifesting, refused to sit quietly during the tumult. Instead, he spoke of telling the truth and listening to one another in love; he spoke of reconciliation, while acknowledging the suffering of some and the joy of others. He immediately engaged lay leaders to work with him in the planning and development of a series of presentations and discussions on the issue. He worked with the lay chair of the adult education committee to frame the series theme around reconciliation, and made all of the sessions available to the general public.

When I met with the chair of the committee and the rector, I understood why their parish had not experienced the divisiveness that some others had. The committee's presentations to the congregation and the wider community had better equipped the parish to engage in difficult yet constructive conversations because the rector modeled this behavior. His leadership conveyed the serious nature of the controversy without taking on the fears and anxieties ensconced in others. He also unhesitatingly supported the chair of the committee in her leadership role.

The importance of prayer was palpable. The post-communion prayer from the Rite II service of Holy Eucharist captured their attitude toward each other:

> Almighty and everliving God, we thank
> you for feeding us with the spiritual food
> of the most precious Body and Blood of

your Son our Savior Jesus Christ; and
for assuring us in these holy mysteries
that we are living members of the Body
of your Son, and heirs of your eternal
kingdom. And now, Father, send us out
to do the work you have given us to do,
to love and serve you as faithful witnesses
of Christ our Lord. To him, to you, and
to the Holy Spirit, be honor and glory,
now and for ever. Amen. (BCP 366)

Their work was sacramental and manifest in their organization and action.

The Discipline of Sacramental Leadership

When leadership is viewed as sacramental, we see the Divine
in our interactions with others, and our meetings with others
as encounters with the sacred mystery of Incarnation. We are
then able to adopt a discipline of beliefs and practices that
allow us to:

- Envision what a healthy congregation looks like, and
  mutually identify and teach the habits and practices
  that will help to achieve this vision, which will enable
  the congregation to maintain health now and long
  beyond the tenure of current clergy.
- Ensure that the internal structural and operational
  systems and activities are aligned with the core values
  of the organization, thus building trust in the integrity
  of leadership and in the organization itself.
- See the parish as a living, breathing organism
  with the capacity for both health and illness, and
  be able to identify and articulate warning signs—
  "symptoms"—of issues that pose a threat to the

health and well-being of the system. This can be accomplished without dividing the congregation into camps "pro" and "con," or isolating those with whom there is conflict.

The Sacramental Practice
of Reading Reality

No matter how smart and sophisticated or capable a leader is, forming too quick an assessment of what underlies troubling symptoms can ultimately lead to work-avoidance and an abortion of the best solution or resolution. Leaders must always allow for other possible explanations that differ from their first conclusions.

Sacramental leaders can step back and gain a bigger view of a system and anticipate the impact that changes will have. It is difficult to see the whole when immersed in a myriad of day-to-day activities. Leaders engaged in transformational change are called to relinquish the managerial tendency to see only pieces and parts rather than the relationship between the parts. The axiom that "the whole is greater than the sum of its parts" holds true for organizational systems.

When the vision is shared, it triggers inspiration, but its implementation becomes the greater challenge. Just as there is danger in pushing people too fast toward a goal to the point that integration of change does not happen, it is equally dangerous to think that once a vision is articulated the work is done. In fact, the point of agreement on a vision is when the real work begins. Keeping the energy and commitment of followers high at this point is paramount, and helping those involved to understand what and how they learned in the process will serve the organization well in accomplishing change in the future. As Peter Senge, author of *The Fifth Discipline,* says, "Most advocates of change focus on the changes they are trying to produce and fail to recognize the importance of learning capabilities." It is the learning capability of a congregation that will enable it to deal with future change and challenges in a healthy manner.

Sacramental leaders seek outside consultation and assistance in reading reality in times of stability and instability. They understand that the capacity to check their own perceptions and their effect on individuals and organizations minimizes the chances for internal eruptions. And when a crisis does occur, leaders and followers have the presence and patience to withstand the pressure to fix the problem before they really understand what the problem is.

The Sacramental Practice of Inner Work

Since sacramental leadership is leadership that is based on self-knowledge, sacramental leaders must engage in the inner work of integrating being and doing. As Richard Niebuhr writes in *The Responsible Self*, "Self-knowledge is no mere luxury to be cultivated during idle moments. It is essential to the responsible life."

Leadership as sacrament recognizes that the primary instrument through which an organization can be freed to use its gifts and skills to change is the selfhood of the leader. It is the authenticity and integrity of a leader that engenders trust and confidence, and inspires shared responsibility and prudent action. These leaders are described as real and "down-to-earth" by followers. Identification with the leader helps followers to be more willing to engage in risk-taking and to do what is needed for the good of the group in spite of the possibility of failure.

There are multiple places in parish cultures where anxiety and fear lurk. What keeps these potentially corrosive emotions at a manageable level is a leader with a clear vision, an understanding of shadow and light, a connection to an overarching purpose, and the capacity to communicate focus and direction. These capacities provide a strong sense of security and meaning to followers.

Creating a community of learning and trust means developing a place in which individuals can risk being real and truthful, a psychologically and spiritually safe place where members feel a sense of belonging and are guided by the knowledge that there is something larger than their self-interest that must be considered. In this spiritually rich environment people can bring their whole selves for healing and growth.

The Sacramental Practice of Leading Change

The sacramental leader understands the processes of change and selects and equips an internal "change team" to assist in bringing about the desired change. This kind of leadership helps develop these individuals into a cohesive group with a shared vision and a plan for strategic implementation of the vision. A planning or change team is united in its knowledge of parish history and of the character and culture of the organization. The lesson to be learned is that every organization has a history of responding to change, and knowing this history can assist the change team to intervene in ways that diminish anxiety and increase trust. It also is a reminder that change is not the enemy; denial that it exists or quick-fix responses are.

If the leader is a facilitator of change, problems are perceived as part of growth and ultimately solvable. In those situations in which the leader is resistive and reactionary, the message conveyed is a lack of confidence in the organization's internal capacity to deal with troublesome issues. The presenting symptoms of a problem can take on a life of their own, fueling more anxiety and enticing the leader to make unwise judgments and responses.

No matter how skilled leaders may be in communication, whatever they normally do will not be sufficient during complex change processes. In understanding the sacramental nature of leadership, they will find many and varied ways to send the desired message to followers that they want internalized and emulated. The leader lends clarity and consistency to the process. If the leader says the organization values open, honest opinions, then those who express themselves openly and honestly should be affirmed for this behavior. When the desired behavior happens, it should be immediately recognized and rewarded.

Sacramental leadership is not easy. It requires a high level of commitment, competence, confidence, and patience. In assuming this mantle leaders will be continually reminded that their real work is never finished. The real work is the development of a community of faith with the capacity to engage in actions and activities that are transformational.

Sacramental leadership is never a solo act. It involves a community of peers and followers committed to the vision, mission, and ministry of the church. The way this happens is through the practice of disciplines that lead to building trusting relationships and honest communication. The ability to create a community of trust and learning is key because the process of transformation is adaptive work, not a static, predictable sequential cycle.

The Sacramental Practice
of Mutual Ministry

Sacramental leadership encourages the practice of mutual ministry, with leaders who truly believe that they have much to learn from others—both laity and clergy. The gifts and talents of many laity often lie untapped while clergy feel overworked, overextended, stressed, and burned out. The gifts of clergy can remain buried or underutilized if the laity hold on to rigid roles and stereotypes of who clergy are and what they "should" do.

Brian Prior, now bishop of the diocese of Minnesota, once served as rector at the Episcopal Church of the Resurrection in Spokane, Washington, and understands these practices well—he could have written them while leading his congregation through large-scale change. Brian was working as a diocesan staff member on congregational development when the bishop informed him of two troubled congregations and the possibility that they could become yoked. When this possibility turned into reality, Brian was asked if he would start the new church.

He did what a leader who understands the sacramental nature and practices of leadership would do. Using the Baptismal Covenant as the core document to frame and guide the process, he engaged the congregation in an in-depth conversation about what they wanted their future to look like. During the listening process he began to hear alignment around a vision: the desire to be known in the community as "a place in which people are faith-fed in order to feed the world." The congregation wanted to be ministry-centered, not clergy-centered, and Brian seized this as an opportunity to create a different model, something respectful of the parish history yet exemplary of freedom to choose a new future. His style of leadership is one of inquiry, and he asked multiple questions to bore down into the cultural level where core values—which are central to the work—reside.

He affirmed the challenges they faced and the successes shared during his stay. No matter what lay members did, Brian helped them to see that "everything contributes to the whole, and everything is ministry!" Whatever the service rendered, he would write a thank-you note acknowledging their ministry to the church and community. These events are not isolated ritual and activity, they are the making of identity and calling. This is leadership-as-sacrament in practice.

This story is a reminder of several things. One is that the *being* of a leader is a critical factor in a transformation. Another is the significance of a leader with self-awareness and a vision of the preferred future. A leader does not always have to be the sole architect of the vision; in fact, his or her role may well be to listen for it within the congregation and then to take what is heard and enable the congregation to bring it to fruition. To do this means using the set of sacramental practices and skills already identified. One that has not yet been discussed but is recognized as necessary by all leaders who understand the sacramental nature of how they lead is the capacity to convene.

The Sacramental Practice of Convening

Congregations are a complex mix of different people, with differences in perspective, education, knowledge, experience, skills, and economic condition. The leader's daunting task is to acknowledge and respect these differences and weld them into a community of a common vision and mission. The skill of convening is a critical practice in accomplishing this.

Convening consists of technical skills such as setting dates and times for meeting, selecting a location, and inviting participants. Developing an agenda, facilitating the proper attention on the right issues, sharing authority, ensuring accountability for task accomplishment, and setting up systems of sustainability are included. Effective leaders learn that these skills are the first order of response in building community. The complex and relational nature of his parish initially surprised Brian, and he quickly learned to use his understanding and knowledge of individual and group development to revitalize congregational ministry.

Whether the group has been in existence for some time or is just beginning, having an understanding of how and why it was formed, its developmental trajectory, and its underlying and operative values and assumptions will equip a leader to be most effective. Convening is a practice that is much more than just showing up; it requires considerable knowledge and preparation on the part of a leader. In order to convene there must be a basic knowledge of group development, group dynamics, and group process. The leader must know the history and composition of the group, know the norms and level of participation and its life in the parish, and use this information in planning the process of building relationships and trust. The historical research will reveal such facts as who envisioned and started the group; what the founding vision was and currently is; how it has evolved to date; what its achievements have been; and what its challenges are.

Knowledge of group development gives the leader an indication of what kind of interventions and behaviors will be most useful in its development. For example, in the early stages of a group's development it is appropriate for the leader to be more directive and to provide more structure. This is usually done by clearly communicating the purpose of the group, its goals, objectives, and desired outcomes. Clear expectations of membership are stated to help people decide whether they can invest and commit. Norms are made explicit to ensure respectful, constructive conversation. An example of group norms we use can be found on the following pages.

GROUP NORMS

1. *Begin and end on time.*
   Whatever times the group has established, they will agree to honor. If it looks as though they cannot do so, they will renegotiate.

2. *Each person is actively engaged.*

Those who attend are committing to a deep level of involvement in the process, which will require listening, paying attention to what is going on, and being actively engaged. This allows each person to participate in the ways they are most comfortable while being cognizant that how they choose to participate positively or detrimentally affects the group as a whole. This also reminds the group of the variety of ways that people can contribute and participate—everyone does not have to talk, and everyone shares at their level of comfort.

3. *Be open, honest, and direct.*

Communication in the group needs to be an open and honest process if the group engages in real work. Each participant is committing to behavior that will create an environment in which this level of conversation can occur by modeling direct, honest feedback themselves.

4. *Use "I" messages.*

This is a corollary to number 3, and provides an important way to honor that norm. Using "I" messages helps each participant to own responsibility for their own thoughts, ideas, and feeling. This does not permit people to speak for others or to hide behind what others may feel or think.

5. *Be respectful of differences.*

Each person brings his or her own distinctive history of experiences and perspectives to this experience, and it is important to acknowledge and respect this in the course of conversation. We are asking participants to listen and respond respectfully, seeking to understand but not necessarily to agree.

6. *Attend and prepare for all sessions.*

This is essential to a group if they wish to fully benefit from this experience. Assignments are to be honored.

7. *We all have expertise.*
   Everyone has considerable knowledge and skill; it is important for us to remember this and create ways in which it can be utilized. This norm diminishes the chances of entrenched hierarchies in a group to remain established and invites the participation of all.

8. *We are responsible for our own learning.*
   This norm is very similar to number 6, but broader. This is a contract with the group to help form the educational experience and to shape what occurs in the session. Participants are asked to speak up if they have questions, concerns, or suggestions or if they are feeling lost or disconnected. The opportunity to renegotiate their experience is always available.

9. *We will keep information confidential.*
   Everything shared in the group remains in the group. If an individual wishes to discuss their own experience, they can but they are asked not to share what others said, did, or decided without the person's consent.

10. *No beepers or telephones.*
    Participants will find the educational experience far more beneficial if the group is not subject to continual interruptions or external diversions. The focus needs to be on the work at hand, and the group needs to know that there is shared focus and commitment and a stability to the membership as they deal with difficult issues.

11. *We can stop the process and confer.*
    This is a norm that allows for anyone to stop the process and ask for clarification or renegotiation of activities based on time or need considerations. This permits a certain level of creative flexibility necessary in good pedagogy. It also heightens participants' ownership and sense of responsibility for what is going on in the training.

12. *Serious work can also be fun.*
   This is not a command, but an invitation and
   reminder. As one of my mentors reminds us, "This is
   a serious business, but it need not be a deadly one!"
   The leader needs to pay attention to creating the
   space and environment for an element of playfulness
   and humor to happen.

Every group establishes rules for how it wants to operate.
To a stranger they may be unspoken and discovered only
through experience. If a leader observes that a group becomes
silent in the presence of conflict or that it rushes to judgment or makes decisions quickly, he or she is observing group
norms. Leaders help groups make their norms for behavior
explicit and lead them to examine, evaluate, comply with,
and/or modify them when needed.

Through observation the leader learns whether a group is
in the first stage of development, during which issues of inclusion and exclusion predominate, or if they are in a later phase
of resolving issues of power and control or negotiating levels of
desired relationships. Any one of these phases is instructive to
the leaders and influences the behaviors assumed.

We have all heard of instances in which there is member
dissatisfaction in parishes. If the leaders respond aggressively,
the members can move into repression or regression, but the
memory of discontent remains, ready to add fuel to another
incident later. Creating a community of trust and learning
requires the cultivation of a culture of dialogue and an ability
to engage others in deep conversation. When group members
feel they can speak their opinions freely and disagree without
fear of retribution, trust grows.

When "hospitable space for disciplined reflection" is created, a climate of psychological trust and safety is established
so that group members can feel free to share their thoughts
and feelings without fear of violation of confidentiality. When

members can trust that what they say will remain in the group and will not be used against them, they feel able to risk being open and honest. The way to help people learn this is to provide a space in which they can voice their opinions and beliefs and also be open to the opinions and beliefs of others without being ostracized or chastised. This is the practice of leadership as sacrament.

The chart on the following page can assist leaders in identifying when they are working on a technical or adaptive aspect of an issue. This model can be used as a tool to examine a parish's preferred model of ministry.

MODELS OF MINISTRY©

	CORPORATE MODEL		MINISTRY MODEL
FOCUS	Metrics	←→	Mission
SKILLS	Technical	←→	Adaptive
GUIDED BY	Strategic planning	←→	Prayerful discernment
PROGRAM DEVELOPMENT	Competitive	←→	Collaborative
GOAL	Growth	←→	Connection
STRUCTURE	Hierarchical	←→	Circular
LEADERSHIP	Authority, status, power	←→	Altruism, trusteeship, passion
CONGREGANTS	Resources for deployment	←→	Resources for development

While the practice, disciplines, and models sound easy, their implementation is complicated by the fact that human behavior is complex, organic, and, at times, unpredictable. This means the leader must always be both observer and participant. What the leader sees and hears will guide whether, when, and how to respond. A key skill of sacramental leadership is the appropriate timing of an intervention. The leader can usually tell when the timing is optimum because the response of the individual or group is less defensive, the real issue surfaces, the entire group is engaged, the conversation is open, and the group moves forward in the real work it must accomplish. The art of reading the group while also mobilizing it to accomplish its work is sacramental leadership. The leader ensures that the diversity of opinion and the wide range of thoughts are expressed and given respectful consideration in discussion and decision-making.

The context, processes, and tools for leadership as sacrament are transformational. They help leaders know when to use technical and adaptive skills. They are able to read the surface and the depth of issues and of parish culture, lead an array of groups through the phases of change, and create communities of learning and trust through modeling authentic leadership and using their knowledge of group development.

Summary

"And now, Father, send us out
to do the work you have given us to do."

This desire to serve expressed in the Rite II post-communion prayer is the heart of sacramental leadership. These are our marching orders, and they convey the notion of leadership as a sacramental act of faithful witness, love, and service that brings honor and glory to God.

The Episcopal Church is at a crevice in history, a crease in time when it is being called to reset and restate in new ways who we are and why we exist. We are being called to identify what we can contribute to resolving the turbulence within and without in transformational ways. We are being called to be a credible and authentic example of Christian faith. We are to exemplify congruence in our beliefs and actions. Our ability to influence and exercise power will be revealed through authentic behavior and integrity of being. Sacramental leadership is rooted in tenets and practices familiar to the readers of this book and found in the previous volumes in this series. There has never been another time in which the potential of the Episcopal Church to change and to lead has been needed more. Our Baptismal Covenant must be the standard for how we work together inside the church and out in the world. We can no longer thrive in top-down stratifications of entitlement in which power *over* rather than power *with* predominates. Leadership as sacrament is our ministry. Information must be accessible to all, and core values must be clearly articulated and aligned with our actions. We cannot sequester people in beautiful spaces of worship, music, and liturgy without also engaging them in deeper reflection on identity and character, calling and congruence. We can practice prayerful silence *and* embrace responsible action.

Robert Kennedy's words remind us that "few will have the greatness to bend history itself; but each of us can work to change a small portion of events, and in the total of all those acts will be written the history of this generation. All we need is courageous leadership." We have this kind of leadership and the potential for more of it exists in the church. Our task is to elicit the "spark of God" and through intentional education and development of clergy and lay leadership set the church ablaze with the passion of the Christian vocation. When we do, reality will shift and all things will be transformed. May we have the courage to heed our call.

Nothing that is worth doing
can be achieved in our lifetime;
> *therefore we must be saved by hope.*

Nothing which is true or beautiful or good
makes complete sense in any immediate context
> *of history;*
> *therefore we must be saved by faith.*

Nothing we do, however virtuous,
can be accomplished alone;
> *therefore we must be saved by love.*

> —*Reinhold Niebuhr*

chapter 2

With Open and Courageous Hearts

Tools for Evangelism

David Gortner

If I speak in the tongues of mortals and of angels, but do not have love, I am a noisy gong or clanging cymbal.

—*1 Corinthians 13:1*

How do we go about the work of transforming our ideas about evangelism and creating an effective spiritual practice of evangelism? Let us begin with Paul's words to the Christians in Corinth, words that remind us we don't have to be extroverts in order to be effective evangelists.

St. Paul's words in his first letter to the Corinthians are about *motivation*—and about people's ability to see through our words to our motivations. People are smarter than we give them credit for. They can often sense when they are being manipulated, conned, or fed an empty performance—and for young people, this is particularly true in their encounters with religion. Conversely, people also know when they are hearing the voice of genuine love, heartfelt honesty, or courageous vulnerability. These are our first tools for effective evangelism: the ability to speak and act with love, honesty, and courage about God's transforming power in our lives. The more we learn to love without embarrassment, to tell the truth to ourselves and one another, and to speak and act in spite of our fears, the more we will become living testaments to God's redeeming work. Evangelism begins with prayer for the Holy Spirit to transform us and teach us these things.

Now, there are more than a few "strategies" and "tools" that won't work—that are turn-offs because they communicate something other than genuine love and joy. Just try these "sure-fire strategies to turn people off" and see how they work for you:

1. Come to our church—we NEED you!
2. See how slick and polished we are.
3. Try Christ—you really need *something.*
4. Come to my church, so that someone else can tell you the story I'm too timid to tell myself.
5. Yeah, I'm not sure how much of all of this I believe myself—but come anyway.

Besides an overemphasis on getting people "in the door" and thus focusing on the institution, these strategies come across as insulting and fail to communicate the deep integrity, beauty, and truth of our own stories of transformation by God's grace.

Too frequently, I have heard and watched Christians rely on the institution through its worship, fellowship, and preaching—or even on the fact that it exists—to tell the stories of transformation that others are ready to hear but that they are too timid or uncertain to share themselves.

This laissez-faire approach to evangelism reminds me of two stories. One is from the television show *The Simpsons*. Ned Flanders, a tightly wound religious soul, as a rowdy child is taken to a psychiatrist by his "lousy beatnik parents." His parents are heard to say, "You've gotta help us, doc. We've tried nothing, and we're all out of ideas." The other story is from a parish I served. When we were considering ways to become a more hospitable place, the congregation was considering new and improved signs and directions in the church building—including signs to the bathroom. Lizzie, an outspoken member who was not particularly happy with some of these changes, said, "Why do we need signs telling people where the bathrooms are? They can always ask someone, can't they?"

Inner Transformation: The First Step in Evangelism

Without inner change, no tools or methods for evangelism will ring true—we will simply be noisy gongs or clanging cymbals. As with the development of any spiritual practices, transformation of behavior begins with a focus on inner transformation. What kinds of inner transformation will prepare us for a profound spiritual practice of evangelism? There are many possibilities we can consider—but here are six.

1) *Self-love.* As Christians, we are seeking and learning to love ourselves as Christ loves us, both our unlovely and lovely parts. We can practice self-love in a waking prayer each morning: "I love you, God, for my being." We can also allow ourselves to be loved by others through times of celebration, mourning, and forgiveness, and when we discover love by loving others.

2) *Self-knowledge.* In ongoing transformation, we develop habits of recognizing and voicing our ultimate need for God and for rigorous but loving self-examination. We have brief opportunities to do this kind of self-examination every week in our confession of sin during the Sunday Eucharist. Clergy can invite the people gathered to reflect more directly on their lives during the silence before confession, and give more space for honest self-reflection. We can also take part in the Prayer Book rite of reconciliation, where we share our confession with another person, lay or ordained.

This kind of honesty with ourselves is attractive to people who have not yet dared to admit to themselves who they are or explore who they are becoming.

3) *Compassion.* Compassion is not pity, but the recognition of another person's full humanity, warts and all. Self-knowledge leads us to compassion through prayerful reflection on our own fallible, fragile, and fleeting lives, and how all benefits in our lives depend on the contributions of many people.

Parishes can assist in fostering compassion by offering outreach programs that employ an action-reflection model, in which people do work (like building a house for Habitat for Humanity) and then return to discuss why they did what they did and what they learned. Parishes can also create an environment of honest encounter with local and international human needs, through periodic videos and invited speakers.

4) *Courage.* Courage, or fortitude, helps us to overcome anxiety and become eager to proclaim the source of our strength and joy. Courage does not mean becoming a bully. Nonviolent protest demands courage to walk or stand in the place of the enemy. Assertiveness demands courage to say what you mean and to speak directly to error. Vulnerability to tell one's own story demands courage. These are habits that congregations can foster. Clergy and laity alike can practice

courage in how they engage conflict and speak the truth about their experiences with one another.

5) *Integrity.* At the close of the Eucharist, we pray for "gladness and *singleness* of heart." Unfortunately, we find it all too easy to live compartmentalized and divided lives, splitting off our religious life from the rest of our lives. And we need not enter this work alone—dedicated small groups help hold us accountable and focus on our single-hearted purpose to live as disciples.

6) *Humility.* Humility emerges with increased self-knowledge and compassion—and it provides a safeguard against false self-love and overly aggressive "courage." True humility involves a recognition that I speak, act, and live as one life, one person with limited but real experiences and perspectives to share in these fleeting moments—and that my unique life does not give me more privilege of voice and action than anyone else. The Amish understand this particularly well in their emphasis on foot-washing as what an outsider might dare to call a sacramental act. Foot-washing, like the exchange of the Peace, is one of the great leveling actions in the church, where each of us is servant, and each of us is served—and both positions take humility.

It is important to note that communities committed to the kind of discipleship that involves these six inner transformations will naturally strengthen their practices of continuing evangelism, as they apply themselves to teaching and training their children in living the Christian faith. "Primary evangelism" will emerge naturally—churches committed to ongoing transformation in the Spirit are going to attract people. Changed lives speak.

Below are a series of questions for exploration by individuals, small groups, and congregations. These questions invite you into loving self-assessment by asking you to identify moments in your life in which you have been learning or experiencing self-love, increased self-knowledge, compassion, courage, integrity, and humility. The questions are meant to open the door to self-reflection, prayer, and the sharing of stories with one another.

Self-Love

- Name a time that you knew you loved yourself. What happened? What did you love?
- When have you been deeply grateful for being you, for your life, for your experiences?
- What do you hold dear about yourself? What do you not love about yourself?
- What does God love in you that you do not yet love? How can you ask the Holy Spirit to be in conversation with that part of yourself?

Self-Knowledge

- When have you seen something about yourself you hadn't seen before? How did you take in that new information?
- In the course of your life, what new has emerged, what has died, and what has remained constant?
- What are your "favorite" or habitual sins—done and left undone?

Compassion

- Who is an example of compassion for you?
- When has your heart stirred with an expansive love and desire to commit yourself to the good of others? What sparked that experience, and what did you do?
- Whom do you love most dearly and whom do you despise? Where are each of them hurting or vulnerable in their lives? Can you hold them and their vulnerability in your heart with compassion?

Courage

- Who is an example of courage for you?
- When have you faced and overcome anxiety in speaking the truth or acting according to your deepest convictions?
- When have you stood up to somebody for destructive behavior?

Integrity

- Who is an example of integrity for you?
- When have you acted with the greatest integrity?
- Have you ever felt divided against yourself, acting or speaking in ways out of keeping with your deepest convictions?
- Who is good at "holding your feet to the fire"?

Humility

- Who have been important examples of humility for you, in history and your own life?
- When have you made a contribution to people's lives and been the least concerned about recognition for your contributions or skills?
- Who helps keep you humble, in the best sense of the word? What does that person do to help bring you back to a different sense of yourself?
- What does it mean to you that Christ "emptied himself" to live and die among us?

Habits for Evangelism

Practicing Gratitude

Gratitude is the fundamental act of worship. Whether in everyday mundane exchanges with others or in our most central act together—celebrating the Eucharist, which means "thanksgiving"—our expressions of gratitude are moments of worship and adoration. As we give ourselves freely to expressing our wonder at the wideness in God's mercies, our lives are transformed into sacraments of thanksgiving for the goodness of the Lord.

The practice of gratitude is not blind optimism, but a mental choice we make. There are famous classroom studies—and more recent studies in business—that have demonstrated the "Pygmalion effect": when a teacher assumes that a child will do well, the teacher treats the child differently, offering more challenges and rewarding performance more vigorously—and the child responds by rising to the occasion. Our practice of gratitude with others helps others see themselves differently. People experience us reflecting back to them that we have witnessed the image of God within them.

To foster habits of gratitude and wonder, individuals and groups alike can use a modified form of the Ignatian examen—a review of each day in conversation with God. Toward the closing of each day, review with God the gifts you received and the joys you experienced. These gifts may be as seemingly insignificant as a smile from a friend or stranger, good basic customer service at a store, an extra hug from your child or a chore done without complaint, a kiss from a lover, or even the trains running on time and the trash getting picked up. Or they may be more extraordinary, like a moment of reconciliation with an estranged family member, an unexpected inheritance, a gift from your parents that clearly indicates their personal sacrifice, or forgiveness from someone from whom you least expected it. Recall whether or not you remembered to express your gratitude in the moment, to yourself, to God, and to the other person. Ask God for guidance and clarity in such moments in the future. The next day, be mindful of choosing at least one situation in which you will be intentional about expressing gratitude directly, in the moment, to another person and to God. This is of course a personal practice, but it can be done in small groups as well—and it works particularly well in families, as a part of the Faith Stepping Stones approach to helping families form habits of faithful Christian practices in their children.

Congregations can learn the habit of gratitude through exchanges of gifts and thanksgiving with one another and their surrounding communities. When clergy and lay leaders start saying "thank you" through notes, e-mails, and phone calls, they often learn that this is the first time some people have ever been thanked for their labors in church.

A neglect of gratitude shifts the spirit of congregational life from gift to duty, from possible source of joy to necessity. How simply we can begin to transform our common life by expressing gratitude to one another. This can extend to gratitude for people in our surrounding communities who help sustain our common life. Imagine how a community might respond to a church that held services, festivals, or dinner celebrations for people who work in all sectors of labor and public service!

It is also possible to help people recognize in everyday life their own moments of deep gratitude. I recently met with a young couple for marital counseling. Neither was connected to the church, but when I asked them how they talked and connected with one another on spiritual matters, Stan perked up and talked about a time in the past week when they were out to dinner. He had shared with Sharon how the moment struck him—that he was amazed and grateful that they were able to enjoy such a pleasure as sharing a meal at a restaurant where they could eat outside in a beautiful environment, and remembering that so many people do not have access to the same delights.

We discussed this moment as a way they had already prayed together, and that this was actually a prayer of gratitude—their "grace" over a meal. They responded with surprise and delight, and agreed to continue these conversations with each other.

Learning to Listen

Developing awareness begins with curiosity about the people around us—both in our individual lives and in our shared congregational life. We begin to pay attention to those in our neighborhood, on the streets, in the stores and malls, among our colleagues at work and school, in the parks, on the playgrounds, and in the clubs and gyms. Like the man in Luke's gospel who wants to inherit eternal life, we begin to ask Jesus, "Who is my neighbor?" (Luke 10:29). As we become more practiced in compassion and gratitude in our everyday lives, we will encounter other people differently—and begin to notice more acutely our own internal barriers in interacting with people who are not like us.

Thus, the next step in effective evangelism is learning to listen. "Evangelistic listening" is deep and respectful listening to the life stories of others and seeking out signs of the presence and work of the Holy Spirit. But it begins with listening to the everyday concerns, experiences, and perspectives of people around you. Evangelism and church growth writers frequently stress the importance of getting to know census data and other sources of information on population trends and other changes in their communities. I agree. There are many such resources that can help a congregation get a better picture of the needs, interests, passions, and changes in its surrounding communities. Sometimes, congregations experience such reflection on "the big picture" as an awakening and a challenge to their sense of relevance and importance in the community.

These kinds of data are only introductions, however, and no substitute for good, honest footwork. You will need to get out and "pound the pavement," visiting shops, parks, coffeehouses, bars, libraries, and neighborhoods, striking up conversations with strangers, and getting to know them and their experiences in the community. This kind of work is integral to learning the practice of a kind of "holy curiosity" about our neighbors and daring to get to know them. It is the only way we begin to enter the work of the incarnate Christ, who "pitched a tent" among us. Truly radical hospitality begins here, with a non-defensive willingness to hear anything, including judgments against God, religion, and church—even yours.

When I am exploring a neighborhood or getting to know my neighbors or new colleagues, I ask questions like the following:

- Where are you from, and what brought you here? Why did you decide to live/work here? What kind of life do you want to have here, for yourself and your family?

- What's your overall impression of this town or neighborhood? What kinds of folks live/work here?

- What would you like to see happen in this community? What is happening here that concerns you? What excites you? What are some issues that are really important to you?

- What are your favorite spots here? Where do you like to spend time?

- What are some things you can do that you like to share with others or offer others?

- Who do you turn to when you need help? Who do you rely on?

- What are the best things about this place? What are some things that concern you?

These and other open-ended questions allow people to respond with stories that give you glimpses of their ideals, yearnings, needs, and passions. Community organizers rely on this kind of listening to understand the needs, interests, and strengths of a community and to help bring people together in networks of common goals. Training organizations like the Industrial Areas Foundation, Gamaliel, and People Invested in Community Organizing teach community organizers how to do "one-on-ones"—conversations with people in their homes and places of work, where they can use their powers of observation to identify what might be core concerns and interests of people. Many pastors and lay people who have gone through this training for their congregations have found their whole way of understanding ministry transformed. Perhaps a picture of a graduating teenager or a book about Mexico on a shelf says something about what is important to a person you are visiting. What can you ask about it?

"Evangelistic listening" does not mean asking *religious* questions. Those can come later. "Evangelistic listening" means listening for the spiritual and theological meaning in what people are telling you about their experiences in your community. When a mother tells you she is worried about bullies on the playground, what are her heartfelt spiritual concerns? What is spiritually important in the story a contractor tells of having to fire some day laborers who were making too many mistakes on the job? When people talk about their community as safe or unsafe, beautiful or run down, healthy or unhealthy, are they saying anything deeper about what they are seeking in life and what they believe is right and good?

It is not difficult to invite people into conversations about their beliefs and values—and it is possible to do this without using "God-language."

Naming the Holy in Your Life

Now we are to the heart of evangelism. The essential step in becoming an effective evangelist is learning to name the Holy, being comfortable naming the moments in our lives when God was most clearly evident to us. We can do this by taking stock of our lives, recalling moments of discovery or new opportunity, difficulty or trauma, celebration, sadness and loss, fear, surprise, profound friendship or solitude, or simply peace and contentment. We can do this by recalling important events, amazing places, and influential people in our lives. And, as we might find it difficult to recall these moments readily, we can help ourselves remember by asking ourselves the same questions we will use with others in spiritual and theological conversations.

But before we can *tell* our own stories, we must come to *know* our own stories. This means that we have to pay attention to our lives as they are unfolding every day, and review the events that have touched us and stayed with us in our personal histories. The "spiritual time line" can be a powerful way to review our lives and put together our stories in new and surprising ways. Education for Ministry (EFM) and Disciples of Christ in Community (DOCC) programs use the "spiritual time line" in a way similar to the following:

1. Take a piece of paper, turn it sideways (or put several papers side by side), and draw a horizontal line across the middle, marking off years of your life in even increments (every three, five, or ten years) starting from birth.

2. Using one color, mark the "highs" (above the horizontal line) and "lows" (below the horizontal line) that you remember happening at different points in your life—"external" events and experiences when you were surprised by delight, changed, stuck in

a rut, or dismayed by loss (such as births, deaths, changes in job, health, and relationships).

3. Using a different color, mark the "highs" and "lows" of your spiritual life—times of closeness to and distance from God, inner turmoil and transformation, meaning and belonging and purpose (or their absence). These may or may not involve church.

4. Tell the story you have drawn on your "spiritual time line" to others in a small group. Each story will take time—allow twenty to thirty minutes. Clearly highlight moments in your life when you sensed God at work. Others in the group listen prayerfully, offering thoughts after you finish on how they sensed God at work in your life story.

Obviously, this exercise from EFM and DOCC is meant to be done in small groups, and will take several meetings together to complete all the stories. But the first three steps of this exercise can be done in solitude as well, as a way of holding one's life before God in prayer.

You may also find helpful another modified Ignatian examen. First, quiet yourself, and become aware of God's many graces. Reflect on the goodness of being and of being loved. Ask for clarity and openness to receive God's guidance as you review some events and experiences of your life. Note any memories that arouse powerful emotions, and hold these emotions before God, expressing gratitude, wonder, sorrow, or anger as it arises. Make note of what struck you in these moments and think prayerfully about how they shaped you.

Coming at things from a different angle, some may find it helpful simply to talk to themselves about God. This may seem an odd suggestion. And yet, with a faith that stresses the incarnational reach of God into the gritty nature of creation itself as a habitation, talking about God should be as easy as talking about an apple, or bread, or a friend. We may simply need practice. So, talk to yourself about God. Let this conversation with yourself become a kind of prayer, where you say to yourself all that you have felt, thought, experienced, or doubted about God. And, to keep the conversation interesting, talk to God about God.

We are free in prayer to speak to God directly and tell God directly what we think and feel. And, just to complete the loop, talk to God about yourself. If we grow more accustomed to talking to ourselves about God, we will likely become more comfortable talking to others about God. Likewise, if we grow more accustomed to talking to God and asking God about ourselves, we will likely find it easier to talk to others—and to ask others—about ourselves. Which brings us, finally, to telling others our own story. When I *know* my own story, I know what I have to offer, and can present parts of my life as a living testament to the love of Christ and the surprising presence of the Holy Spirit.

Your Most Sacred Christian Stories

Each of us has Christian stories or passages from Scripture and tradition that we treasure—stories that enrich, expand, and undergird our understandings and experiences of God. We can practice telling these stories and passages to ourselves and others, and practice connecting the stories of our own lives with them. This is at the heart of Christian spirituality and witness, and is lively in many African-American and Native American Christian traditions.

Your most sacred Christian stories might include tales and narratives from the Bible—the days of creation, Abraham bargaining with God, Ruth following Naomi, Nathan confronting David and David confessing, or Jesus at the wedding at Cana, teaching Nicodemus, feeding thousands of people, or healing the lepers. You may have favorite poetic passages from the Psalms or other Wisdom literature, the prophets, or the New Testament hymns to Christ. You may be stirred by stories of saints through the ages, like those of Francis of Assisi or Julian of Norwich, Dietrich Bonhoeffer or Martin Luther King Jr., Dorothy Day or William Stringfellow. There may also be "secular" songs, stories, and movies that express for you core gospel themes of God's relationship with humanity and humanity's search for God. Many in my generation found powerful expressions of the gospel in the music of U2, the Indigo Girls, and Cake, and in movies like *The Mission, Shawshank Redemption,* and *The Matrix.*

At age two-and-a-half, my daughter Cassie had a favorite Bible story—the parable called "The Lost Sheep." When we brought her children's Bible to church or got it out to read at dinner, she asked for that story, and for "The Really Big Picnic" (the feeding of the five thousand).

One day we stopped by the Sonoma Mission—the northernmost Spanish mission in California. When we went into the chapel, Cassie wanted to climb up the steps of the pulpit. I explained what the pulpit was for, but that we couldn't use it, since it was roped off. She said, "All right, I'll stand here and preach." She proceeded to tell the story of the shepherd and the lost sheep—and then continued with the story of the woman and the lost coin. She then asked me to take a turn preaching the same story.

Some biblical stories and passages have become very much *mine* in how they speak to me and for me. During a tumultuous time in graduate school, in the midst of conflict with a faculty advisor, I was worried that everything was going to collapse around me—that I would lose my research position and project, and that I would possibly not be able to continue. I came home to my apartment, sat down, and opened the Psalms. I came upon Psalm 63 (BCP), and my eyes became fixed on the verse that reads, "My soul clings to you; your right hand holds me fast." I closed my eyes and began to pray that verse over and over again, breathing in and out with each phrase. I felt steadied, calmed, and re-centered. For over a year, that verse was my daily "mantra." At first, I prayed it for myself. Then I found that I could pray it for others as I encountered people throughout the day. I still return to that verse as a clear expression of my yearning for God and my hopeful trust that God will hold me.

One of my favorite phrases in our liturgies comes up only once a year, at Ash Wednesday. I remember the moment when the words "Remember that you are dust, and to dust you shall return" changed from something I anticipated with solemnity and anxiety to something I received gladly as a gift. I came to a point where I was grateful for my mortality and happy to be reminded of it. I now find myself smiling at the moment when a priest says the words to me and I feel the slightly rough rub of ashes on my forehead. I am glad that this life—for all its joys and troubles—has an end. I do not want that end to come too soon. But I am grateful that I do not bear the responsibility of more than this one life, so I can embrace the responsibility and gift of this life more fully. The Word of God speaks in new ways to me and for me as I live the fullness of my life, and I find my own story interweaving in new ways with the Great Story of God's redemptive work, reconciling presence, and passionate love relationship with humanity and all creation.

Where Is God in Your Neighbor's Life?

Now comes that risky but wonderful practice of naming the Holy in someone else's life, bearing witness to what we perceive as the presence and work of the Holy Spirit. Admittedly this takes practice, and must always be done with humility as well as courage—for instance, "You know, Sarah, God seems to have been guiding you," or "Paul, maybe God is already having some conversations with you—what do you think?" But it is not nearly so daunting if we have spent time and effort cultivating our other evangelistic spiritual practices by which we develop natural habits of sharing our own stories and allowing them to interweave with the great stories of Christian Scripture and tradition. The more natural and easy we become at naming our own experiences of grace, the more naturally we will find ourselves naming the Holy in other people's lives—a profound, intimate gift that strengthens bonds of human affection.

It is possible that someone will reject the notion of God at work in her life, at least at first. But be alert: someone's seeming rejection may be accompanied by a quizzical look that might be asking, "Do you really mean that? Are you for real?" Don't simply withdraw your naming of the Holy— you might even gently and pleasantly persist, suggesting once again that God may indeed be at work. As someone accepts this possibility or is at least considering it, you may be surprised by the different reactions he might have. Laughter of recognition, thoughtful silence, quiet tears, a sigh, a smile, a scowl of deep thought: all of these are responses that let you know that your gift has arrived and been opened.

We should not rush rashly into such profound space, but neither should we retreat from such encounters simply out of fear of walking on holy ground. Naming the Holy in others' lives requires discernment, courage, vulnerability, and deep respect—the kind of response required of Moses in response to God's invitation, "Take off your shoes, for this is holy ground." The process of this evangelistic practice is simple, really—which does not mean that it is simplistic or easy.

There are three things we do: 1) Listen; 2) Pray and adore; and 3) Speak. Listen first. It is too easy to skip or minimize this crucial gift we offer in evangelism. When the urgency to speak strikes you, ask yourself first, "Have I truly heard? Have I listened to the heart of this person's story?" When the temptation to give up or ignore a story hits you, ask yourself, "What am I missing?" Intent and focused listening brings us into contact with things people may not even be aware that they are saying—and lets people know that we are genuinely interested in their lives.

We listen not just with our ears, but with our eyes, our bodies, our souls. The more deeply we listen, the more we will hold up a mirror to others, allowing them to see themselves in new ways. Can you repeat the story? Did you catch the change in vocal inflection, the smile, the shift in posture? Did you follow emotions where they led? Are you able to summarize, to play as it were a short film documenting what you have seen and heard? Can you ask the questions that allow more to be revealed? These are the signs of profound listening.

In the midst of listening, questions will occur to us: *What was the turning point? How did God break through? Is this person hearing how he talks about this important moment in his life? Where are the signs of God at work in the imagination, motivations, feelings, and actions of the people involved?* These questions can become our prayers, that the Holy Spirit open our eyes to see Christ at work. When we recognize the marks of God in someone's story, then we may dare to name the Holy: "Jan, I believe you met God in that moment." "Jason, God is at work in your life—can you feel it?" "Thank you, Sarah—you have shown me Christ." This is by no means a casual or tentative statement; it is a moment of profound but simple worship and proclamation.

Families are a natural first place to practice. Imagine how different our interactions with teenagers—and with parents— would be if we entered such conversation with one another at least once a week, inviting Holy stories and being prepared to name the Holy in each other. We can model this for our families and guests at various gatherings, like holidays, cookouts, and receptions. And, as so many families find themselves getting locked into patterns of seeing and naming only the negative in one another—or in taking one another for granted—there is a great ministry for us to embrace, to offer ourselves as "surrogate" grandparents, children, and family members who will speak words of wonder, joy, and adoration.

Once you have offered this gift to someone, allow the person some time and space to respond. It may also be helpful to offer a piece of your own story, or a story from Scripture or Christian tradition, to help someone through this powerful and vulnerable experience. It is a good idea to ask permission to share your own story or something from Scripture. "May I share something that your story reminded me of?" It may help someone to connect the dots and see something new and unexpected in her own life.

Congregations can engage more explicitly in naming the Holy by marking and honoring major transitions in people's lives. Such transitions include those traditionally marked in church rites—baptism, marriage, and burial—where opportunities for naming the Holy extend well before and after one liturgy or prayer. But there are a host of other transitions in life that can be marked by times of public prayer, blessing, and acknowledgment of change: graduations, relocations and moves, job changes, and retirements are all worthy of community prayer and recognition. Other significant transitions, such as births, engagements and marriages, and deaths, afford multiple opportunities *beyond* church rites and liturgies for the community to name the Holy and bless the people involved.

What Happens Next?

The preparation is done. We are forming new habits and practices with our faith and discovering the wonder and delight of hearing and telling the stories. Now comes that next major step: stepping out from our safe enclave, becoming the pilgrims we really are, and bringing our stories of gratitude and wonder into our day-to-day interactions with people. Now is not a time to return to fear and anxiety. Now we must remember our practice of allowing ourselves to be in the grip of gratitude—for it is our gratitude that propels us out to a waiting world.

God goes before us. "Grandmother" Kaze Gadaway offers advice on how to help people develop this awareness as a habit: "One exercise I had the young people do was to go out onto the streets of Holbrook and look around—and ask, 'Where is God here?' And, you know, they found God in all sorts of places. Once they had done this the first time, they were excited to do it again. So I sent them home with the same question to ask through the week." Beginning with "Grandmother" Kaze's lead, it is a simple matter to begin talking to people we meet, inviting them into conversation and inviting them to talk about themselves. Most people experience our interest and curiosity as a gift—and, while they may be initially surprised by questions that invite them to share important life experiences, most respond gladly to this opportunity to talk about things they usually don't get a chance to share. It can be helpful to remember some of the "evangelistic questions" outlined earlier in this chapter, to help focus our conversations. If we can allow ourselves to respond to the lure of God that tugs us out into our communities, fueled by our gratitude and excitement of discovery, God will become as much a natural part of our public and private discourse as food, and we will need no more gimmicks or buttons or tracts or catch phrases.

In our neighborhoods, we can engage in regular periods of "coffeehouse conversations"; small groups from congregations can spread out in a community, going to coffeehouses, parks, clubs, and bars and can begin conversations with people through the practice of evangelistic listening. Young people may be able to help us relearn the freedom of speaking naturally about our faith in the midst of everyday conversation. Instant messaging, e-mail, and website conversation spaces like Facebook have allowed people to find new freedom with each other in conversation. With the power of partial anonymity, people talk about themselves with surprising openness.

Religion and faith enter conversations alongside food, music, relationships, and work. A few years ago, I was playing backgammon online. My opponent was a single mom in Pennsylvania. Between taking our turns, we chatted—and I started talking about my involvement in church. She started asking me questions—and she trounced me in backgammon because I kept forgetting to take my turn while I was thinking about how to respond to her!

Regular practice within "coffeehouse conversations" will reveal new ministry opportunities and help the congregation connect more deeply with its surrounding community. My seminary students get the same assignment every year: to go out and talk with individuals they do not know, practicing evangelistic listening, and to bring back to the class what they learned. One student had this to say about it: "On the day we went to do our interviews, the whole way into the city, David, we were cursing your name! I mean, we really didn't want to do this. And then, when we got to the street corner where we were going to go our separate ways to do interviews, we stopped and prayed, 'Oh, Holy Spirit, help us!' And, we went and did the interviews—and we were, each one of us, transformed. We were stunned at how much people were willing to share."

With practice—and only with practice—anxiety gives way to anticipation and enjoyment. When we become this comfortable in our own "Christian skin," we will find ourselves face to face with people in moments that call for our full proclamation of the gospel. Such moments may come after many conversations and shared activities or they may come quite suddenly, at the outset of a conversation or in a situation calling for intervention. While we can never prepare fully for such moments, we can remind ourselves of what it means to care so much about the gospel that we cannot wait to sell it, share it, or give it away. We can thank God for our passions and excitement that help us let others know what we care about and want to share with them, asking for the Holy Spirit's clear voice to ring out from within us as we seek to proclaim good news to a hungry and thirsty world.

"Come and See": Inviting and Following Up

Our evangelism culminates with an explicit invitation—to come with us on a journey, to learn and experience more on the Way, to seek God with others who are seeking. As pilgrims we tell people of the places where we have found Christ, and we invite them to join us. When this moment of invitation comes, we want our faith communities to be prepared to respond effectively with its full roster of fellowship, programs, ministries, worship, and proclamation.

The practice of invitation is a spiritual discipline that involves all members of the faith community. When inviting others to "come and see," we want our invitation to be warm and clear, our welcome to be genuine and hearty, and our follow-up to communicate our gratitude and fond remembrance. There are some basic principles that can strengthen congregational practices of invitation, hospitality, and follow-up. These principles have been used by various churches, and are core guidelines in church planting, programs like Theology on Tap, and congregational development:

- *Four points of contact.* According to market researchers, people need to see or hear an announcement at least four times before responding to it, and ideally in four different ways (such as personal contact, flyer, postcard, e-mail, advertisement). Multiple ways of announcing and inviting give you the advantages of breadth and repetition.

- *From the familiar to the unfamiliar.* The best word-of-mouth approaches emphasize starting with people you know and contexts you inhabit and moving out from there to less familiar people and settings.

- *From personal to impersonal.* Personal contact sticks with someone longer, so the personal invitation is always best. If you are going to use multiple points of contact, lead with personal contact. Face-to-face is stronger than a phone call, which is more personal than a written note (but not if you leave a message!), which is more personal than e-mail. The impersonal contacts of mass mailings, radio spots, print ads, flyers, street banners, and website postings still reach some people, but the personal invitation needs to take the lead.

- *The 1:4 ratio.* In the Theology on Tap model, each young adult who serves on any parish's planning team commits to inviting four people who typically don't go to church. This is a great model: a successful evangelistic event depends on the invitational work of its planners, and by following the 1:4 ratio, a planning group ensures that the event will be well-attended (a planning group of five, for example, can expect at least twenty to twenty-five people total). It clearly gives people who are planning or creating an event the responsibility and opportunity to invite friends and neighbors. It also guarantees that the people who are invited will know at least one person when they arrive. And it keeps the focus on people who are new rather than on church "regulars."

- *Crying out in the marketplace.* A different but powerful approach is that of "Grandmother" Kaze with Navajo and white youth in Arizona, Bonnie Perry in Chicago, and students from The Office at SUNY-Buffalo. These evangelists met people directly in homes and on the streets, boldly announcing what they were there for, and being insistent and persistent in the face of initial opposition or suspicion. When you have something really good to offer, there may be times to blast it openly in public.

- *Clear directions and signs.* When I arrive somewhere, I like to see well-marked signs for parking, room locations, and restrooms—what adult wants to have to ask where the bathroom is? I also like to know that there are clearly identifiable people I can ask for help.

- *Multiple introductions.* People generally respond well to meeting more than one person at a new place. As Chuck Treadwell practices in McKinney, Texas, we can think about who we would like our invited guests to meet. Who has some common interests or experiences? When we introduce our guests to four or five people, we think about points of connection.

- *Clear self-description.* Congregations that are clearer about who they are and what they do uniquely as disciples are more likely to have a sense of vitality and energy. This clarity is also attractive to people—people like to make informed decisions about groups with which they associate. Part of being hospitable is being clear about who you are as a community.

- *"Improbable conversations."* John Dreibelbis, my colleague at Seabury, watched in congregations for how often people who might not usually connect found each other and engaged in conversation. Are older people talking with teenagers, and vice versa? Are people of different races or economic status talking together? The more freely people talk with each other in a community across obvious categories, the more a stranger will be intrigued and be able to imagine a place for himself.

- *Invitation to give.* Not everyone is drawn first to a community because of what they receive; sometimes it is more important for someone to sense that they have something to give, to contribute to the community. Like Susan Sherard did at Holy Spirit in Mars Hill, North Carolina, people in your community can help visiting pilgrims find groups and experiences where they can express their gifts, longings, and passions.

- *Human connection around the rites.* Marriage, baptism, and burial bring people into contact with faith communities at significant moments in their life pilgrimages. Individuals and couples in a congregation can befriend these new pilgrims in the months or days before the rite and stay in contact with them long after the rite. A periodic personal card or call from the church, particularly at anniversary dates and other important seasons, connects people's individual journeys to the life of the church.

- *Personal thank-you contact.* If you extended the invitation, extend personal thanks, face-to-face. A personal note of gratitude from someone in the community echoes your personal thanks. Congregational ministries of invitation, hospitality, and follow-up involve all members. But some members will show themselves as more invested and gifted in this evangelistic work. It will be wise for the church to invest its time and training with those who are gifted, passionate, and invested in evangelistic work, for they will lead our church's efforts at that most-needed and effective grassroots level. Congregation leaders can watch for people who have a natural affinity for evangelism or a passion to learn—and invite them personally to become involved in leading the congregation in evangelism. This is what John Cusick calls "The Jesus Method of Organizing": not seeking disciples by posting a flier or an announcement, but directly inviting people face-to-face.

Older, more established congregations and ministries need to support these new "faith ventures" vigorously so that they have the best chance possible of reaching people who otherwise are not interested in darkening the door of a church. Whether these ministries take the shape of café churches, new monastic communities, social and community-building ministries, or groups committed to new faith expressions through arts and technology, they can only thrive with sufficient support and investment of trust from older members, and established congregations.

And Now for the Programmatic

I have made the case throughout this chapter that we need to turn toward more individual and interpersonal forms of evangelism and not rely on the institution to bear the full responsibility of proclaiming the good news. People respond to *people*. People respond to personal stories and direct expressions of wonder and joy. Without these personal connections, people may experience the church's worship as irrelevant.

But now it is time to come full circle. The worship, programs, and gatherings of the whole congregation bring together the many disparate individual stories of God's transforming love to bear on one great story. In communities of disciples aware of their own gratitude, the story of God's redemptive work in Christ becomes a living story. In the journey of conversion, many people find their experiences in church—hearing a sermon, praying the eucharistic prayer, singing a song, watching people interact with one another, or praying or working with others—as a kind of "tipping point." Through church programs and corporate gatherings, people often come to a moment when they say, "Ah, yes, it is really true" (or, sadly, "I'm sorry, but I'm just not seeing it"). Below are some brief reminders of important evangelistic work that congregations can do.

1. Welcoming, Hospitality, and New Member Incorporation

A ministry of welcome and hospitality means attentiveness and warm receptiveness to the stranger—and a constant remembrance that we are there for others and not solely for ourselves. Programmatic solutions to the need for welcome and hospitality tend to feel programmatic, both to congregants and visitors. But if enough individuals in congregations adopt newcomer welcome as a specific way to practice their overall evangelistic spiritual discipline—"meeting my neighbor"—then welcome and hospitality become integral expressions of a congregation's spiritual life. Newcomer welcome is a perfect place to practice evangelistic listening and naming the Holy. As individuals engage in "meeting their neighbors" at church, conversations lead to people sharing their interests and affinities with each other, and it becomes easy for newcomers to find people with whom they can explore their own sense of meaning and contribution.

When meeting someone, it is not necessary to ask if he is new to the church. You can simply begin conversation, asking him about life and talking about your own life.

Some churches have adopted this strategy by printing "coffee-hour topics" in each week's bulletin. Suggestions of affinity topics for conversation help people connect to one another in new ways—long-term members and newcomers alike. This levels the playing field and takes the pressure off welcoming by simply drawing people into conversations with each other: "How many siblings did you have in your family?" "What were your most memorable holiday traditions?" Congregations will become livelier simply by fostering these kinds of conversations between people, as members and newcomers alike make new discoveries.

2. Preaching, Teaching, and Small Group Encounter

At the heart of Christian proclamation, instruction, and fellowship is our hope that we and others will witness, recognize, name, and celebrate the Holy in our lives. Sermons, classes, and groups give people ways of interpreting, reframing, and redirecting their own thoughts and motivations. It is time to begin a shift toward a more evangelistic focus in the pulpit. Most fundamentally, this involves expecting people to show up who do not yet know God's love or the basic stories.

An evangelistic focus in preaching involves: 1) unapologetically speaking truth in love; 2) giving up the assumption that we are preaching to an in-crowd, instead committing to clarity by explaining up-front our hidden or over-rehearsed Episcopal scripts; 3) helping people see and rediscover their encounter with the living Christ; 4) including newcomers and strangers by acknowledging their perspectives; and 5) demonstrating that it is possible to name the Holy, in our own lives as well as the lives of others, and daring to offer our own witness to the wonder and fallibility of being human and to God's grace in all of that humanness.

Teaching events are most effective when they include time for small group discussions in which people can interact with themes by speaking from their own experiences. Small groups vary in purpose and duration, but recent small group models have stressed the importance of a group covenant having purpose, duration, open membership, and a pattern of prayerful self-disclosure and shared midrash on each other's lives as places of the Holy.

3. Service: The Action-Reflection Model

Only some people will be drawn to faith or hear God's invitation to new life in sermons or the rites of the church. Many youth and young adults are more drawn to communities and groups where they feel they can make a difference in the world. It is powerful for volunteers to meet together and share their experiences with each other and with a broader group of people. It is also powerful for people serving and served to come together to reflect on their experiences of grace with one another.

The action-reflection approach can be part of our unique offering to any public work in which we participate. This action-reflection process can add a new and rich dimension to the "deeds-based evangelism" for which our church is known. As much as possible, our service ministries should be publicly advertised, open to public participation, and in cooperation with other churches, businesses, and religious and social organizations.

4. Worship and Music

Worship tends to be one of the "hot buttons" in any discussion of evangelism, renewal, or church growth. People have clear ideas, whether right or wrong in a given context, about what is most inviting or evangelistic—which may have more to do with their own attachments and revulsions than with a primary focus on offering God's good news in the clearest, most evocative way.

At the end of the day, it is not clear that one form of worship or one style of music is superior as an evangelistic witness. Ancient or modern, plebian or proletariat, strictly by-the-book or wildly novel—it is possible for any form or style to be delivered well or poorly. I have served six different congregations as an organist, choir director, and music ensemble leader, as well as a priest, and I have helped direct liturgical planning in three different congregations.

I have seen problems and blessings with all forms.

People make basic judgments about worship when they come to a church: Is there *passion* and is there *quality*? In other words, do people seem to believe what they are doing or saying? Do congregation members seem engaged or bored? Is the liturgy smooth and natural, clear of haphazard uncertainties? Does the worship clearly communicate the gospel from beginning to end? Is music performed and led well, and does it draw people into deeper prayer and worship?

Most essentially, when planning and evaluating worship, teams should ask, "Is our worship getting across with any power to the stranger in our midst?" This kind of question challenges us to consider ways to introduce moments of surprise or startling clarity into our liturgies and music—which can become reawakening moments for all the faithful.

5. Sacramental Life Transitions

People come or return to churches at significant moments of transition in their lives and the lives of their families. We mark some of these moments particularly in weddings, baptisms, and funerals. For weddings, many churches require the couple to worship regularly and get involved in classes and events. Most clergy require a series of premarital counseling sessions, although these vary widely in quality and focus. More importantly, there is opportunity for follow-up with a couple after the wedding, through personal check-ins, invitations by individuals and groups to gatherings, and cards at anniversaries.

Heather and I went through an intensive birthing class before the birth of our first daughter. As we watched rather remarkable videos and talked about very intimate details of the birth process, we formed a kind of community with people in the class. Every class concluded with a "spiritual moment" of passing a candle around and saying what in the class was important that week. Heather and I found ourselves wondering why churches didn't have these kinds of classes, where the sense of community could continue beyond the end of the course and beyond birth.

With funerals, there are many missed opportunities for follow-up with family members and friends—and this cannot be the sole work of ordained ministers and church staff, nor can it fall on a few volunteers. When my mother died, members from the Evangelical Mennonite congregation we had joined came in a steady stream for weeks with food and friendship. I remember being so grateful for that outpouring of love and care—and also wishing later that people would have continued to check in with us, as it took me over a year to awaken fully to my grief. Churches can learn from hospice organizations about the best ways to be with people in grief, over months and years of bereavement.

In all these moments of sacramental life transition, evangelism is a continuing ministry of bearing good news to others through our gifts of presence and friendship, sharing our stories, and walking holy ground with people who may not yet know how profoundly holy it is.

New Ways of Thinking

As a final note, there are some movements in the church that challenge us to think in new ways about evangelism. They include seeker services, house church, the Emerging Church movement, New Monasticism, and church planting, as well as web-based communities and evangelistic efforts. It would be easy to commit an entire chapter or book to each of these movements, in which committed clergy and lay leaders work together to create new approaches to corporate worship and expression of Christian faith—with the central aim of freeing God's good news from clichés and tired routines so that it may be heard afresh by people who do not yet know how much God loves them.

Some may wish to dismiss these efforts as simplistic, market-driven, over enthusiastic, or spiritually shallow. But behind these very different methods and approaches lies one common commitment—making the saving and ennobling work of Jesus Christ known to people who would not usually choose to darken the door of a typical institutionally habitualized church. The Church of England is beginning to embrace partnership with these movements and efforts across the United Kingdom, allowing the church to have a much more fluid life with many new expressions such as alt.worship, Base Ecclesial Communities, café churches, cell churches, midweek congregations, community-organizing faith communities, seeker churches, and youth and young adult congregations.[2]

There is a concept at play in these approaches that can be a bit unnerving to our institutional structures and attachments: "unleashed ministry." These new types of communities—as well as many of the communities of faith described in this book—practice a kind of "unleashed ministry," where

---

2 *Mission-Shaped Church: Church Planting and Fresh Expressions of Church in a Changing Context* (London: Church House Publishing, 2004), 44.

lay people and clergy alike are set free to develop and pursue ministries of their choosing, both inside and outside the church. Such freedom generates excitement, sparks imagination, and encourages a spiritually enriching examination of assumptions. All this leads to communities of people offering a powerful witness to the profligate, effervescent generosity of God through the Body of Christ.

Rick Warren, in his definition of a seeker service, may offer the best summary of contemporary efforts. He has identified three "nonnegotiable elements of a seeker service: 1) treat unbelievers with love and respect; 2) relate the service to their needs; and 3) share the message in a practical, understandable manner. All other elements," Rick concludes, "are secondary issues that churches shouldn't get hung up on."

The focus on "keeping it real" in these new church gatherings means that the conversations and worship expressions may seem a bit gritty, as sacred and profane meet in sometimes surprising ways. But Rick Warren also offers an important observation. "A service geared toward seekers is meant to supplement personal evangelism, not replace it. People generally find it easier to decide for Christ when there are multiple relationships supporting that decision."[3] In other words, evangelism depends most fundamentally on us as individual Christians living out our Baptismal Covenant to proclaim God's good news by word and example and to find and love Christ in each person. How much we are willing to embrace these elements of our Baptismal Covenant as our core spiritual passions will free our hearts and minds to be as creative, resourceful, and attentive as we can, so that we may follow wherever the Holy Spirit may lead us.

---

3   Rick Warren, *The Purpose-Driven Church: Growth without Compromising Mission* (Grand Rapids: Zondervan, 1992), 246–247.

chapter 3

Making Disciples

Linda L. Grenz

Go therefore and make disciples of all nations, baptizing
them in the name of the Father and of the Son
and of the
Holy Spirit, and teaching them to obey everything that
I have commanded you. And remember, I am with
you always, to the end of the age.

—Matthew 28:19–20

The transformation of Christian discipleship in the Episcopal Church is rooted in this Scripture passage from Matthew's gospel, which is often called "the great commission" and represents Jesus's parting words to his disciples. Transformation begins as an evangelizing process which initiates a lifelong journey of growth in one's relationship with Christ, culminating in baptism. It continues in baptismal living as part of the body of Christ, the presence of Christ in the world. The task before the Episcopal Church is twofold: both preaching and teaching, evangelism and catechesis.

"The Church is called to engage in an evangelizing catechesis, which not only communicates and nurtures the life of faith, but unceasingly confronts and continually converts those within and without the community of faith to gospel loyalty, convictions, and commitments."[4] Out of this mandate have emerged key theological perspectives that challenge how the church engages in its ministry of formation.

The Baptismal Covenant

The restoration of the baptismal liturgy to Sunday morning and the focus on the Baptismal Covenant has probably done more than anything else to shape the Episcopal Church since 1979. While most of the attention focuses on the five questions after the creed, I want to begin at the beginning—with the renunciations and affirmations.

> Do you renounce Satan and all the spiritual forces of wickedness that rebel against God?
>
> Do you renounce the evil powers of this world which corrupt and destroy the creatures of God?
>
> Do you renounce all sinful desires that draw you from the love of God?
>
> Do you turn to Jesus Christ and accept him as your Savior?
>
> Do you put your whole trust in his grace and love?
>
> Do you promise to follow and obey him as your Lord?

---

4   *Called to Teach and Learn: A Catechetical Vision and Guide for the Episcopal Church* (New York: Episcopal Church Center, 1994), 19.

The task of evangelizing catechesis is, first and foremost, to help people develop a relationship with Christ that empowers them to turn away from evil and sin and turn to Jesus. In the early church (and in some congregations today), candidates at baptism would literally turn 180 degrees—from facing west to facing east—signifying a totally new direction in their lives. This is, at the end of the day, the heart of what the church is about—accepting Christ as our Savior, putting our whole trust in him, and promising to follow and obey him.

We are called, not just to tell people *about* Jesus, but to help them form a personal relationship with him. We are called to form people as Christians—as people who are not just "believers" but people who are in relationship with God-in-Christ. The church is the body of Christ—the community of those who have been baptized into Christ's death and raised with him into new life. This is more than giving intellectual assent to a set of beliefs. It is even more than living a good Christian life, engaging in Christian practices, and contributing to Christian causes. It is a relationship and a commitment to "follow and obey."

One of the challenges we face today is finding ways to present "follow and obey" so that this message sounds like Good News to modern ears. We live in a time when many people want to lead or want to be independent—free from the influence of anyone or anything. And while that freedom is illusionary (we are all influenced by something and someone), it is a value many people hold dear. Add to that the need to "obey" and we are in real trouble! It is hard to find anyone who is looking for someone to "obey"—a word with largely negative connotations in our culture. So it is no wonder that we quickly slide through this part of the service before happily settling on those much more comfortable five questions after the creedal affirmations.

I think we need to reclaim and perhaps reframe these commitments. For example, "obey" is a word that comes from a combination of *ob*, "toward," and *oedire*, "to hear."[5] So "obey" might be understood in our age as hearing the Word and moving toward (following) where it is leading us. We need to see obedience itself as a process of formation, a process of being drawn into a deeper relationship with Christ and, in the journey, being shaped more and more in his likeness.

Christian formation is a process of being sanctified, of being made holy. This is not something we do by ourselves—it is God's action. But it is in our turning away from all that separates us from God and in our turning toward Christ and choosing to walk in this path that we open ourselves to God's act of sanctification. We do not become Christians by learning *about* holiness; we are gradually formed and transformed into the holy people of God. That process begins before baptism, but God's inward and spiritual grace becomes visible and real when in the midst of the gathered community of Christians we renounce all that separates us from God, turn to Jesus as our Savior, and promise to follow and obey him.

Immediately after the renunciations, the entire Christian community recites the Apostles' Creed, which articulates the core beliefs of the Christian faith. Creeds are difficult for many people: they were written a long time ago and use language and images that are foreign in today's world. It is clear that most of us are not alone in our discomfort with at least some of the words or images in the creed.

There is an educational activity that has been done in churches and conferences that highlights this ambivalence. The leader asks the participants to listen as the creed is read slowly and stand up when they believe the words without

5   From the Merriam-Webster dictionary: Middle English *obeien*, from Anglo-French *obeir*, from Latin *oboedire*, from *ob-* toward + *oedire* (akin to *audire*, to hear).

reservations, sit when they don't believe, and hover in between if they are unsure. The end result is that there is much bobbing up and down as people visually signal their comfort or discomfort with different statements in the creed. The point to remember is that the creeds are the creeds of the *church*: as individuals each of us might not understand or totally believe this or that line. But the creed is the church's affirmation of its faith. There are times in our lives when we might not believe much at all—and others in the community believe on our behalf. At other times, we are the ones who carry the church's beliefs for others.

When we stand to affirm our faith in the words of the creed, we stand as a community. When we are baptized, we are baptized into that community—into the body of Christ. We don't all have to have an unreserved faith and believe everything without doubts to be part of that community. In fact, the reason we are part of the community is that the Christian faith is communal. Our faith is worked out in community. We come to faith and understanding of the creeds, of Christ's life, death, and resurrection through our participation in the life of the Christian community.

In the catechumenal process, an adult baptismal candidate walks with a group of Christians who serve as his or her companions. This journey may take weeks or even months as the candidate asks questions, participates in the community's life, and learns what it means to be a Christian. Baptism for the catechumens generally occurs at the Easter Vigil. The journey then continues in a phase called *mystagogy,* which means the interpretation of mysteries. This is the time when new Christians are invited to "go deeper," to reflect on and learn from their experience of baptism. And, not surprisingly, this is the time when they explore the beliefs in the creeds at greater depth. The creed has a different meaning for you *after* baptism than before—and its meaning will shift as you continue on your faith journey.

Baptismal Affirmations

One of the most popular aspects of the 1979 Book of Common Prayer are the five questions after the creed. They capture in succinct, clear language the essence of baptismal living—of what it means to live as a Christian on a day-to-day basis. These questions also have been influential in shaping people's understanding of the church's ministry and the place of both clergy and laity. As individuals become aware of their vocation to proclaim the gospel, to seek and serve others, to strive for justice and peace, to continue in the church's teaching and prayer, then they stop looking for the clergy to do these things on their behalf and start doing them in their daily lives.

**Will you continue in the apostles'
teaching and fellowship, in the breaking
of bread, and in the prayers?**

This first question assumes that everyone, both newly baptized and those affirming a baptism of many years ago, are engaged in learning and worship together. "Will you *continue*" implies that you have already been learning and worshiping in the Christian community. Being baptized is not the end to the journey; it is just one step along the way. The Christian is called to continue to learn, to participate in the life and worship of the Christian community. Christian formation happens in community. Most of us "catch" the values, beliefs, attitudes, and practices of the Christian life from those around us. We learn by listening, seeing, and doing. Before the apostles had any teaching to pass along to us, they spent years walking with Jesus and absorbing what he did and said. The Christian life today is no different. We learn from each other. And we learn by teaching. Unfortunately we learn negative behaviors just as easily as the positive ones, so it is important to reflect on our experience, to hold it up to tradition and the Scriptures to see where we are aligned and where we are not aligned.

Continuing "in the breaking of bread, and in the prayers" highlights the role of worship in the Christian life. Christians are called to give thanks for all God has given us, to receive spiritual nourishment and intercede for others. The weekly celebration of Eucharist is the community's expression of being the body of Christ. In it we are renewed to go forth and carry out our ministries in our daily lives. We are nourished both by word and sacrament. And we bring our concerns for others to God in prayer.

The liturgy is where our lives as Christians scattered are united with our lives as the Christian community gathered. In our participation in liturgy, we are formed as Christians in many ways. Some are obvious: the Scripture readings and sermon teach, inspire, and encourage us. Some are not so obvious: the hymns imprint images, phrases, and understandings of God on our hearts. (It is often said that people's theology is shaped by hymns more than anything else.) We are also formed in liturgy by very subtle things—the action of bowing when we approach the altar or an ambry with the Sacrament present embeds in us a sense of the holy and heightens our awareness of God's presence. The rhythm of the liturgical seasons mirrors the rhythm of our spiritual journey. The oil used to anoint us in a prayer for healing opens us to God's healing action in our lives.

Liturgy and fellowship are as important in forming Christians as the traditional learning experience. We need to find ways to be more intentional about engaging people in liturgy in ways that are formational. And we need to value the formational character of our liturgy and our "fellowship" as well as our teaching.

Will you persevere in resisting evil, and, whenever you fall into sin, repent and return to the Lord?

This question probably gets the least attention of all. We don't like to focus on our brokenness, so we give our assent to the question and move on. But there are great opportunities in this question for helping people think about and learn ways to resist evil. We begin by helping them identify what *is* "evil" and to become comfortable with talking about sin in non-defensive ways.

An example: When congregations try to begin a conversation about racism, identifying where it is infecting their lives as individuals and as a community, often those discussions quickly turn into a painful emotional experience that leads them to avoid the topic in the future. We need to learn how to talk about racism calmly. We need those among us who can model acknowledging racist actions without getting defensive or trying to justify or mitigate it. We need to recognize that racism is one of the evils of our time, that we are all infected with it and affected by it, and that we all need to be working on resisting this evil. When we fail, we need to repent and turn to Christ to forgive, renew, and sustain us as we continue our struggle to resist this evil. There are many other examples—degradation of God's creation, violence, destructive anger, and so on—but racism is one evil that is shared by all of us. The churches in America could well provide a leadership role in our nation by being communities that intentionally work on resisting this evil, repenting when we fail and then getting up and working on it again.

Will you proclaim by word and example the Good News of God in Christ?

We tend to parse this question in such a way that "proclaim by word" becomes a clerical role (preaching and teaching) and "example" becomes a lay role (daily living). But the question doesn't do that—and gradually people are coming to realize that *all* of us are called to proclaim both by word *and* example. This does not mean we all have to take our turn at delivering sermons! But it does mean that we all need to find our voice—our way of articulating the Good News of God in Christ.

For some of us that means talking with our children or other family members at home. For others it may be speaking to a friend or coworker. Still others are called to proclaim the Good News to strangers as they go about their day-to-day lives. Proclaiming the Good News does not need to be a sermon—or the street corner ravings of a religious fanatic. It simply means being aware of God's presence in a situation and being willing to offer God's word in a way that points others toward God. That might mean a simple comment, a thoughtful response to a question, or a willingness to share your faith story. Talking about God with others—*especially* outside the walls of the church—is a powerful formational experience. Learning how to express our faith, practicing ways of doing it, and gaining the confidence to do it in times and places where it isn't expected can strengthen our own faith as well as the faith of those who receive our words.

Proclaiming by example is much easier to envision. We are happy to ladle soup at the soup kitchen, help out at the church's yard sale, take sandwiches to the homeless sleeping under the bridge, or take up a collection to help the needy somewhere in the world. We understand that this is the word in action. And it is fine to "just do it." But often we blur the lines between being good citizens doing good works and proclaiming the Good News by example.

I suspect that's why the question has "by word and example." If we are to proclaim the Good News, we need to *proclaim* it, not just hope that the recipients figure it out. We don't need to push religion or do all of those aggressive things that make us Episcopalians nervous. But we do need to learn how to share our faith, speak comfortably about God and Jesus, pray with others, and be open to or even initiate a conversation about religious matters.

Will you seek and serve Christ in all persons, loving your neighbor as yourself?

Serving others has been a practice of Christians from the very beginning. We often involve children and youth in service activities, with the understanding that this helps form them as Christians. Seeking Christ in those whom we serve and loving everyone isn't quite as easy or obvious as it might seem. We tend to think of ourselves as "bringing Christ" to the poor souls at the soup kitchen, rather than going there to encounter Christ who is already present in those whom we serve. Too often we focus on helping others in a way that merely reinforces our superiority. We have all these good things in life and these poor souls have so little—let us give them a little from our largesse. We then end up doing service as a subtle way of making ourselves feel better ("There but for the grace of God, go I").

This approach to serving others forms us, but isn't appropriate Christian formation. When we are able to shift from the charity model (I have, you don't, so I help you) to a compassion model (we are companions on the way), we can see Christ in the face of the other. It is in those moments that service is transformational. When we seek and serve Christ in those we meet, we encounter the risen Christ—and our acts of service become holy. If we seek Christ in our serving, we soon realize that serving others is a privilege because in doing so we are blessed by Christ's presence in them. Christian service forms us as humble servants of Christ.

"Loving your neighbor as yourself" makes this an even more challenging question. Loving our neighbor next door, a family member, social friends, and even coworkers is not a huge problem. But loving the stranger on the street who is acting decidedly strange, loving the person who is mean or even violent, loving someone who has done some great harm to you or loved ones is a much tougher proposition. Christ calls us to love our neighbor, to love the people we encounter in our lives—no matter who they are or what they've done. Love them as fellow children of God. This basic Christian practice of loving others is a foundation stone in Christian formation.

Will you strive for justice and peace among all people, and respect the dignity of every human being?

The last question highlights the Christian's call to work for justice, peace, and dignity for all God's children. We are called to go beyond alleviating the symptoms (hunger, homelessness, drug abuse) to addressing their root causes.

While Christians are often good at passing resolutions calling for justice and praying for peace in the world, actively working for these things is another matter. Effective Christian formation equips us to look at the bigger picture, to see the patterns that create dire consequences for some people while protecting others. It needs to give us the courage to fight injustice, to right those wrongs even if it means we will lose some of our power, wealth, or position. Striving for justice and peace forms Christians by doing—everything from writing letters, crafting legislation, or speaking up in a meeting. Providing occasions for people to reflect on their experience and to recognize their call to strive for justice and peace is an important part of forming Christians.

The Theology of Baptism

One of the major changes initiated by the 1979 revision of Book of Common Prayer was the restoration of the ancient understanding of baptism as the definitive sacrament of full inclusion in the body of Christ. Because the early church primarily baptized adults, men and women were usually baptized and confirmed in the same ceremony. As the church grew and bishops were no longer able to be in multiple churches on Easter Eve (the preferred time for baptisms), priests began doing baptisms and confirmation, which was an integral part of baptism. The emphasis was on baptism and Eucharist and, in the first four centuries, the church didn't use the term "confirmation" as a separate rite.

I believe that in the coming decades, for the first time in our history, adult baptism will become normative in the Episcopal Church. We will still baptize infants, but with a rapidly increasing number of unbaptized adults in our communities, adult baptism must become a regular occurrence as well. This means we need to rethink the rite itself.

The current practice assumes that the baptismal candidate is an infant, so we have tiny baptismal fonts where the priest can hold a baby over it and sprinkle water on the baby's head. These fonts work for babies, but think about an adult being baptized. He must bend his head over the font awkwardly while a few drizzles of water run down his neck and into his eyes. Embarrassing, uncomfortable, and perhaps even annoying—but hardly a powerful or meaningful symbol or experience. It is not unlike the seminary joke about needing a double measure of faith when receiving the Eucharistic bread in the form of a wafer: first you have to believe it is bread, and then you have to believe that it is the body of Christ. First you have to believe that this embarrassing ritual is a water bath that signifies a profound cleansing and even drowning to be raised to new life, and then you have to believe that the baptism is transformative.

If we want adults to seek baptism, we need to make that experience as powerful and meaningful as we possibly can. The baptismal action needs to be "writ large" and fit an adult. The churches that have retained the practice of full immersion have something to teach us: for them baptism is a powerful act that embodies the dying and rising to new life in Christ. While some Episcopal churches are installing immersion pools, this is likely to be a slow change in our architecture. But that doesn't have to stop us from working with adult baptismal candidates to explore ways of doing a baptism that helps that person truly experience being baptized instead of just "sprinkled."

Some congregations have used temporary pools to do immersion baptisms. Others pour a whole pitcher of water over the candidate's head—which requires a larger vessel than most baptismal fonts. While this requires some logistical arrangements (such as providing a bath towel to dry off afterward), it is more likely to feel like something significant has happened than a few sprinkles on the head.

Baptismal Formation

Looking at Christian formation through the lens of baptism should have resulted in education that is different from the models of education practiced in secular society. Unfortunately, even the best efforts of Christian formation in the church are still largely based on secular education models of teaching content and fail to form Christians whose lifestyle is radically different from what it was before their baptism. The revision of the Book of Common Prayer, the expansion of ministry roles to include more people, and the move from education to formation were steps in that direction. But by and large, church is still a congregation and not a Christian community—that is, a gathering of people who *congregate* at a particular time and place to worship God and receive the benefits of his mercies and the church's ministries. They are congregations gathered around a minister instead of being ministering congregations. They are a people who are consumers of religion instead of the people of God, empowered to be a powerful witness to Christ in the world.

Because our culture and circumstances do not naturally incline us to turn to God, we need to find a way to articulate the faith through real and powerful connections to daily life. Ironically, despite our occasional pessimism, the Episcopal Church is ideally suited to meet the needs of this current age. Young people, for example, are drawn to mystery, mysticism, and spirituality. Our liturgy fundamentally incorporates those elements and, with minor tweaks, can easily and authentically respond to that need. Icons, candles, incense, chanting, silence are all things we can encourage that are already part of who we are. Individuals who are willing to spend hours in a yoga class or with a guru learning to meditate can participate in Taizé services, teach meditation methods for Christians, practice centering prayer, and follow the Prayer Book offices of daily prayer.

We can broaden our traditional ways of talking about stewardship to include environmental and health-conscious concerns, encouraging the support of local food sources and helping people develop a respect for their bodies as part of God's creation. The church can foster an understanding that good stewardship means taking care of "our selves, our souls and bodies"; we can help people develop more balance in their lives, highlight the value of Sabbath time, and encourage practices that reduce or eliminate stress. We can build "green" churches and offer them as intentional "teaching churches" where others in the community can come to learn about how to incorporate different technologies into their buildings.

In order for Episcopalians to live into the "great commission," we need to go to where the people are instead of always expecting them to come to us. There are several successful models of people taking the Eucharist to the homeless and general public or engaging people in discussion and even worship services in a local restaurant or bar. The emerging church movement has reinvigorated the concept of house churches and expanded it to neighborhood churches that meet in schools or other public places. We need to take some risks and try different environments and different ways of taking the church to the people. We need to create multiple ways for people to become a part of the Christian community—through worship, learning experiences, service, prayer experiences, and more. In each case, we need to create intentional ways to invite people to move from their entry point into full participation in the life of the Christian community. We need to be intentional about building these Christian communities, even if it means giving up some of what we know as "church"—perhaps even our church buildings. At the same time, we need to find ways to use our buildings to serve the community at large instead of being solely an occasional sacred space for a handful of people.

These are only a few suggestions for how we can begin to move toward a participatory faith—a worship and congregational life that engages people fully, where people are "belonging, being, and serving." Instead of coming to church just to *get* something, people will come to church to *give* something (love, praise, witness, wisdom) and they will leave church with even more to give. People who are full participants in the Christian faith and life gather to give God praise and thanks, to love one another, to serve in Jesus's name—and in the process they are transformed by Christ, again and again, to be the people of God in the world God has created and the world in which they are called to be Christ-bearers.

Making this move means building relationships in the congregation that nourish people spiritually, relationships that empower them to risk living in Christ, relationships that encourage worshiping, learning about, and serving God and each other in new and enlivening ways. We must help people catch a vision so they will risk moving from a life in which they are just going through the motions to being fully *alive*. When new people walk into our churches, they need to feel the power of God's presence in a real and tangible way. They need to be enveloped by a sense of God's love and experience the profound joy of the Christian community.

Every congregation needs to find its own way, but the heart of the matter is that we need to raise our expectations for what it means to be a Christian. Today many of our congregations have a lovely worship service, nice programs, and friendly fellowship—but it is like music being played so quietly that you have to strain to hear it. We don't have to change what we do in radical ways, we just need to turn up the volume. Worship with more investment, risk opening ourselves to God's presence, actively engage in the spiritual practice of loving—even, and especially, those we find hard to love. Perhaps then, instead of finding us fighting about fine points of liturgy or about whom we ordain or about whether our leaders have passed the right resolutions or not, people would enter our churches, discover that we disagree radically with one another, and yet still be able to say, "See how they love God and one another. What an amazing place! This is none other than the house of God!" *That* would be a radical witness to the power of God's love to unite us in faith.

Baptismal Teaching

The restoration of the baptismal liturgy to the principal feasts of the church and the main Sunday service has probably transformed the life of the church more than any other change in the 1979 Book of Common Prayer. What had become a largely private, family affair is once again a central liturgy in the life of the church. Reciting the Baptismal Covenant, and especially the five questions after the creedal affirmation, is changing our self-perception, giving worshipers a succinct summary of a vision for faithful Christian living. As congregations repeat the Baptismal Covenant over and over again, people begin to internalize these questions. On some level, they begin to ask themselves: How am I doing these things? How might I do them more fully, more faithfully? How can the church support me in doing them? How can we help our children and youth do these things *now*—not just when they "grow up"? How can we "live out" our Baptismal Covenant?

Despite some bumps in the road, the journey toward baptismal living has undoubtedly engaged a broader range of people in the active life of the congregation. The church's liturgies generally involve a host of people in various leadership roles beyond the former "choir and clergy assisted by acolytes" model. Many congregations have moved from having committees that make decisions and raise or administer money to coordinating ministry teams that carry out the ministries.

The Baptismal Covenant also became an important formation tool in re-visioning how ministry was carried out by congregations and the roles of clergy and laity in doing ministry. Instead of seeing a largely passive congregation gathered around a minister (who did the ministry), the vision became one of a ministering congregation—a vital congregation, actively *doing* ministry. Those congregations study and pray together to discern what ministries they were called to carry out as a congregation and who among them had specific gifts for ministry. These congregations take seriously the passage in Ephesians that in the church "some would be apostles, some prophets, some evangelists, some pastors and teachers, to equip the saints for the work of ministry, for building up the body of Christ" (4:11–12).

Together those called to these roles along with others in the congregation form a ministry support team and covenant to an ongoing process of learning together. These teams become the primary pastoral leaders in their congregations. They sustain the congregation's life and support the congregation's members as they identify and exercise their ministries in the church and in the world. In other words, their role is "to equip the saints for the work of ministry, for building up the body of Christ."

The development of local ministry support teams solved a growing problem of how to staff small, rural churches, thus increasing their attractiveness in dioceses that were finding it difficult to fund full-time or even part-time positions in these churches. While the underlying theology is one that sees the whole people of God engaged in carrying out the ministry of the church, thus upholding the vision for baptismal ministry to be the model for the whole church, the reality is that money matters. If a congregation can afford to maintain the old "vicar of the village" model of ministry, it is likely to do so. Expanding that congregation's perception of themselves as a community of ministers in their village will require many more years of education about and formation in ministry.

Responding to the Cultural Shift

"Do not be conformed to this world, but be transformed by the renewing of your minds," the apostle Paul urged the Christians in Rome (Rom. 12:2a). The Phillips translation says, "Don't let the world around you squeeze you into its own mould"—a picture that conveys more vividly what Paul meant. The world a person lives in has the power to form and shape us. It is like the wisdom parents like to give their children about choosing friends: "Choose wisely, because your friends make you who you are."

Christians are more likely to find themselves responding to overt or implied questions about their participation in a faith community. As children and youth learn about other faiths from their friends and ask questions, parents are struggling to understand, honor, and explain the differences between faith groups. And as Christians fragment into smaller groups with distinctive theologies and practices, and fundamentalist Christians challenge the faith and beliefs of other Christians, Episcopalians have a growing need to understand and become articulate about their faith. At the same time as there is an increased need for Christian education and formation, there seems to be less time available to do it.

It is easy for the church to adopt cultural values, attitudes, and practices without even realizing it is doing so. The church can get caught up in trying to do more and better programs in an attempt to meet the demands of consumerism. It can lower its expectations and adopt an attitude that says there are no demands of the gospel—just "God loves you and we love you" and that's about it. The church can adopt the cultural pessimism and enter a state of quiet depression. Or it can react to the culture with manic false optimism, ignoring the evils and brokenness that people know is present.

The good news is that the culture also has formed people who are hungry for community and relationships, for meaning, creativity, and spirituality. They want to make a difference. They are open to and eager for what the church has to offer. The church needs to help people understand and use the positive elements of the culture without being "sucked into" those elements that are detrimental to personal or family life—or do not support Christian living. We need to help people see that Christian living is about relationships—our relationship with God, each other, and ourselves; relationships that are in and through Christ. Congregations need to help people find meaning and live out their faith in ways that make a real difference.

If we fail to inspire and support people in their relationship with God in Christ, we risk having the Baptismal Covenant merely add yet more items to everyone's "To Do" list, which ultimately leads to burnout. If we burden people with things to do instead of helping them enter into a transformative relationship with Christ, they will end up being conformed to the culture instead of transformed by God. If we fail to form people as Christians—as the people of God living a radically different lifestyle—we will consign them to being formed by and conformed to the culture. The challenge the church faces today is providing a vision of another way of being and inviting people into a community that shapes and supports their life in Christ.

Reconciliation and Wholeness

Today's world is becoming increasingly fragmented and complex. Many people today seek to understand and respect the perspectives, practices, and beliefs of others. This, obviously, is a difficult stance for someone accustomed to a theology that says that Jesus is *the* way, *the* truth, and *the* life. How can that be true if it is not true for everyone at all times and in all places? Postmodernity says that it can, in fact, be true for you (the Christian) and at the same time not be true for the Muslim, the Buddhist, or the atheist.

In the midst of fragmentation, chaos, complexity, and conflict we are called to be reconciled and to be reconcilers. The mission of the church—that is, God's mission that the church, as the body of Christ, embodies—is "to restore all people to unity with God and each other in Christ" (BCP 855). That mission is rooted in relationships: we are called to be "at one" with God in Christ and to be "at one" with each other in Christ. Being "at one" with God and each other in Christ is both individual (my baptism, my baptismal ministry, my relationship with God) and communal (our congregation's mission, ministry, and relationship with God). A relational theology of reconciliation is both inherently Anglican and amazingly appropriate for the age in which we live. "God, who reconciled us to himself through Christ, . . . has given us the ministry of reconciliation" (2 Cor. 5:18). Our process of "making disciples" must help people be reconciled and become reconcilers in a world that is increasingly broken and alienated.

In the church we often speak of reconciliation and justice as if they were a single act. But the desire for reconciliation and peace almost inevitably collides with the desire for justice. The reality is that reconciliation is needed when there has been something that broke a relationship—and in that brokenness there is pain and real suffering. While forgiveness is an element in reconciliation, there is also a desire for justice. "Forgive and forget" is not enough; those who are injured deserve justice.

So how do we carry out the ministry of reconciliation? While Christianity offers the difference between retributive justice (which seeks to punish in proportion to the crime) and restorative justice (which focuses on the relationship and the need to make amends), the church also tends to focus on the "feel good" aspect of reconciliation and rarely teaches us how to ask for forgiveness or make amends. This may be one of the negative consequences of the 1979 Book of Common Prayer. In its legitimate move from the 1928 Prayer Book's theology of "miserable offenders," the 1979 Prayer Book minimized our sinfulness and the call for confession and contrition. The focus was on the goodness of the created order, especially all of God's children, and on celebrating the gift of Christ's life, death, and resurrection as salvation for all people. Yet it is possible that in making that shift, the 1979 Prayer Book has contributed to the modern tendency to avoid acknowledging and taking responsibility for one's participation in breaking relationships—a necessary prerequisite to reconciliation.

Christian formation must help Christians learn how to be reconciled and to how to be reconcilers in an increasingly complex and fragmented world. This means creating environments in which people can be reconciled to God and each other in Christ—and helping people reflect on and understand that experience so they can be effective ministers of reconciliation. Creating such environments is more than just talking about reconciliation. It means challenging people to see the brokenness in their own lives and to see how we all participate in societal brokenness.

While people may be willing to acknowledge a broken relationship with God, with others in their lives, with themselves, or even with creation, they are often unwilling to recognize their participation in communal brokenness. Because we are part of the human community, all of us participate in the brokenness of the "isms" (racism, sexism, and so forth), the actions of our nation when we kill others (even in "justified" wars), and in the degradation of God's creation. The fact that I may believe that I have not have done anything specific to contribute to societal brokenness does not allow me to escape from being a part of the brokenness. The "sins of the world" surround us and, like the air, we breathe them in and they become a part of who we are. If we are to be reconciled to God we need to first acknowledge our own brokenness, and then seek forgiveness and amendment of life.

Once most people come to accept the brokenness in their lives, it is easier for them to seek forgiveness than it is to amend their lives. We often "talk a good line" in church. We talk about reconciliation, forgiveness, peace, and justice during the service and in our programs—but then we go home and continue life as usual. We forget that true reconciliation is transformative, that it radically changes how we live and move and have our being. If reconciliation is atonement (at-one-ment) then being restored to unity with God and each other in Christ makes a real difference in how we live our lives, do our jobs, and relate to our family, friends, and neighbors.

The task of Christian formation is to help people understand that reality and to create environments in which transformation can occur. Reconciliation is a Christian formation task that takes honesty and investment in building relationships over the long haul. Reconciliation is not a "quick fix"; restorative justice requires more than just spending time with each other. How do we form Christians who are willing and able to pay the price needed to be a part of God's mission of making people whole again?

The theological imperative of the Baptismal Covenant has affected and will continue to affect the life of congregations and shape the way to "make disciples." When the vision of being a Christian was to attend church, pay one's pledge, help out occasionally, and be a good citizen, the process used to form people took one particular shape. Now the vision of Christian living is to be full participants in the congregation's life and ministry—*and* to do ministry in daily life, to proclaim the gospel in word and deed, to seek and serve Christ in all persons, to strive for justice and peace among all people, and to respect the dignity of every human being. Preparing, equipping, and supporting people in fulfilling that vision requires a much more extensive and intensive process than we have used in the past. If we are to "make disciples" who will fulfill this vision, we will need to continue to develop Christian formation programs and materials that are not just educational, but transformational.

chapter 4

The Vital
Congregation

James Lemler

In this chapter we lay the foundations for becoming a vital and growing congregation: the essential work of clarifying mission; being a place of spiritual transformation; becoming aware of the surrounding context and congregational dynamics; the importance of learning and education; and focusing on evangelism and welcome.

Clarifying Mission

The twenty-first century is the "mission age" for congregational life and ministry, theologically and practically. One of the primary characteristics of vitality for congregations is the mission focus and clarity to be found within that congregation. Theology and practice must be joined together in strong congregations where the mission comes first.

This does not happen without intentional care and attention. Every congregation, and particularly its leadership, must pay attention to the understanding and articulation of its mission. Some of this is theological and biblical work, requiring the consideration of the themes of mission from Holy Scripture and doing theological reflection on the meaning of mission in the life and ministry of God's people. Some of this work roots the mission of the local congregation in wider understandings of mission, be it the Baptismal Covenant or the broad definition found in the Book of Common Prayer "to restore all people to unity with God and each other in Christ" (BCP 855).

Attention to mission also involves very specific and particular work emerging out of the experience of the local congregation. Good structures are available to help a congregation in doing this work. Three dimensions of mission mirror God's presence and action over time: the past mission, the present mission, and the future mission. To understand the unique mission of a given congregation, it is essential for leaders to spend time considering all three.

The Past Mission

A congregation needs to understand its past mission since the time of its founding. The identification of historically significant people and events allows present leaders to understand how mission has emerged and developed over time. This is essential to understanding and defining the present mission. History has power in the present, and every congregation is shaped by the decisions and vision of the congregation in its history. Whole congregations can reflect on their history through times of intentional learning and celebration.

The Present Mission

The present mission of the congregation is the embodiment of its values and actions in the present moment. Different congregations have different identities and expressions of mission because of the unique realities of their own values and actions. Values are the enabling beliefs that inspire the congregation to service and actions. A cluster of these values are at work in every congregation. They may be values of learning or lively worship or compassionate outreach. They may be values of inclusion or vigorous invitation or close, nurturing community.

Values are at the very foundation of congregational life, and, to understand mission, the congregation must connect with and understand these values, the things that are "precious" to them, as leadership scholar Ronald Heifetz puts it in his book *Leadership Without Easy Answers*. The second part of the present mission work, then, is to connect a congregation's values to its actions. Is there alignment and resonance between the things that a congregation identifies as possessing great value and significance for them and the actions of the congregational life and program? Sometimes there is an unfortunate disconnect. At other times, there is a proliferation of congregational programs at the expense of effectiveness.

Congregations try to do too much, doing programs that are not rooted in core values or doing such a great number of programs that the congregation's human and financial resources become exhausted. Conversely, when there is resonance and alignment between values and actions, powerful mission can occur within the congregation. Leaders in the congregation have the special charge of reflection on present mission, its values, and its actions. They need to invite the wider congregation into that reflection, though. Some congregations opt to utilize learning presentations of the present mission so that the wider congregation can be aware and help to shape the mission.

The Future Mission

The third dimension of mission lies in the future. A congregation's mission will proceed into the future, and the present mission lays a foundation for the future.

Leaders in a congregation need to dream the dreams for the future and spend intentional time envisioning that future. Congregations can do this in different ways and using different processes. Good visioning resources exist and serve congregational leadership in envisioning a hopeful future and beginning the planning and strategy necessary to enter that future. Mission is composed of all three of these dimensions and directions. The essential thing for a congregation is to reflect, focus, and articulate mission rather than to be distracted by the numerous changes and issues that emerge in parish life. Yes, issues need to be addressed, but even more important is the mission work. Congregations that do this work and focus on their mission are stronger, more resilient, and more able to deal with the inevitable conflict that will occur from time to time.

Questions for Your Congregation

1. How is your congregation doing this mission of reflection, definition, and articulation?

2. In what ways are your congregational leaders spending intentional and consistent time working through all three dimensions of mission?

3. How well are your congregation's members able to describe the primary mission and identity of your congregation? (Mission is more than a "mission statement," but a clear articulation of mission that is understood and used by congregational members is helpful. The important thing is this: you understand the mission, remain focused on it, and use it as a

compass for the progress of the congregation's life and ministry.)

4. Have you used appropriate external consultation to assist in this focus on mission clarity and purpose?

A Congregation's Story

St. John's Church was basically a happy and whole community of faith. It had served its community for almost 150 years and had known many seasons of life and mission. Its town was not large, but it was the regional center of medical and other services for the area. Averaging around 180 worshipers each week, it enjoyed financial health and good community visibility. St. John's offered a number of programs, although many of them seemed to be "running out of steam."

There was something nagging at the clergy and lay leadership of the congregation. Yes, they offered good worship and there were no serious conflicts, but there seemed to be no real focus to what they were about. Neither congregational members nor people in the larger community could identify the core sense of purpose and identity for St. John's.

The clergy and wardens went to the diocesan annual clergy and wardens conference and heard a presentation about congregational mission, inviting them to follow a process as leaders that would give them clarity about mission, a vision for the future, and the beginning of a strategy. They decided to use the consultation offered for their own mission and vision work. The congregation's leaders (clergy, vestry, and some other key lay leaders) invested the time to look at all three directions in mission. What they discovered was of great use to them. They had a rich history, and they learned that past leaders had made some significant decisions that changed the focus of the congregation. They also learned that there had been some very challenging times when leadership had stepped up to the plate to refine and strengthen the congregation's mission. In their consideration of St. John's present mission, they reflected on the values and actions that were at the heart of their ministry. They also examined their community's demographic data and opportunities for mission and created surveys for their own congregational and community constituents. Finally, they envisioned the future for their congregation and began work on strategies and goals to live into that vision.

The result of this work was greater clarity about purpose and mission than St. John's had previously known. The clarity of mission made it easier to attract new lay leaders and volunteers. The new short and pithy mission statement they created became a focused articulation known by leaders and parish members. They began new initiatives, especially in evangelism and stewardship, and "retired" some programs that no longer served their needs. These efforts required a lot of work, to be sure, but a sense of energy and purpose permeated the parish life and culture. They were being transformed and became a more effective congregation of transformation in their community.

Experiences of
Spiritual Transformation

Vital congregations are communities where people can experience spiritual transformation. This happens in several different ways and through a variety of practices. People are transformed through intentional spiritual practices, through worship and prayer, through learning, through Christian community, and through compassionate service (to name some of the major avenues for transformation). The point is this: people yearn to experience a closer connection to and relationship with God.

Spiritual transformation is one of the primary purposes of the Christian church. A local congregation is at its very heart a community and system of such transformation. People come into the gathered community from their daily life and work in the world. They hear God's word, offer praise and prayer, learn together, and have experiences of Christian community. This, in turn, strengthens them for return to daily life and work where they live their ministry in a concrete and continuing way. It is a system of transformation, of change.

Every congregation needs to do an assessment of its life and programs in terms of spiritual transformation. It is not enough to offer something simply because of ongoing custom.

Questions for Your Congregation

1. *Worship.* Does your congregation's worship allow for silence as well as sound? Is there a joyful spirit that engages the worshiper's mind and heart?

2. *Preaching.* Is the preaching evocative and inviting for worship participants? Does it lift up Holy Scripture and connect its proclamation to daily life?

3. *Learning.* Are there sufficient learning opportunities in your congregation? Are they more than an intellectual endeavor (as important as the expression of the mind is), offering spiritual practice and content?

4. *Service and reflection.* Are there opportunities for service followed by reflection on the meaning of that experience?

5. *Spiritual practices.* Are spiritual practices encountered, taught, and encouraged?

6. *Encouragement for all ages.* Does the congregation offer spiritual enrichment for children, young people, and adults?

A Congregation's Story

St. Timothy's is a small and lively congregation in the heart of an American city. It has been a financially supported congregation for decades. The building, built for a large congregation in the late nineteenth century, is far too big for the present average Sunday attendance of fifty people. Over the years the congregation has maintained regular worship and done a few, significant ministries of community service.

A new vicar appeared at St. Tim's who had a passion for spiritual formation and worship. She worked with a group of parishioners who had similar interests and began to develop worship and program offerings to introduce spiritual practices. The worship space itself was changed to be a more intimate and altar-focused setting. New forms of worship and music from the Iona and Taizé communities were introduced, along with expanded use of the liturgies in the Book of Common Prayer, *A New Zealand Prayer Book,* and *Enriching Our Worship.* Silence was employed in worship in an intentional way, and sermons were focused on spiritual growth and renewal.

The congregation began to learn about spiritual practices through reading and experimentation. One person introduced a centering prayer group that also practiced *lectio divina.* A study group read *Practicing Our Faith: A Way of Life for a Searching People* by Dorothy C. Bass and looked to see how these practices were experienced in their own lives and in the common life of the community. Connections to spiritual retreats and resources were offered in person and online as the congregation's website took a new form.

Today St. Tim's is a vital congregation that is just beginning to grow. Its growth is interesting in and of itself. Adults (and a few with children, but not many) have continued to be a part of the St. Timothy's community. There is a steady stream of adult visitors, but there is also a new group that has begun to show up in the congregation. Young adults, college students, recent graduates, and graduate/professional school students have arrived on the scene. Their point of intersection is the sense of spiritual inquiry and transformation that marks the congregation. The congregation is being transformed, and those who participate indicate that spiritual transformation is their primary reason for being present.

Awareness of Context
and Congregational Dynamics

No congregation lives its life in a vacuum. Vital congregations are aware of this fact and seek to learn about the context and environment in which ministry takes place. These congregations also examine their own mission and life in light of learning offered regarding congregational dynamics.

There are several ways of learning more about context and environment for congregations and their leaders. Some of the most effective involve intentional and direct communication with people in their external community. Here are some that congregations have found particularly effective:

1. *Inviting community leaders and neighbors in.* A congregation can use regular program times like adult education for learning conversations with neighbors. Community representatives and leaders are brought to these occasions for presentation and conversation. Congregations also benefit from presentations by community organizations in these learning settings.

2. *Formal community surveys.* Models exist for congregations to prepare formal surveys to learn from neighbors, businesses, and community organizations. Less formal modes of community interaction and survey occur as congregational members are trained to visit neighboring residents, businesses, and institutions for conversation with them.

3. *Public documents.* A great deal of community contextual and environmental research is happening around congregations all the time. This research is undertaken by community and educational organizations. It is readily available but often not considered or addressed by religious organizations.

4. *Public forums.* There are external opportunities for congregational members and leaders to learn about the present realities of their community through participation in community forum settings.

Congregational Size

One of the most important frameworks used to understand congregational dynamics is congregational size. This framework is a particular contribution of the former congregational development director of the Episcopal Church and the first director of the Seabury Institute, Arlin Rothauge, whose pamphlet *Sizing Up a Congregation for New Member Ministry*[6] has become a classic in the area of congregational dynamics. The size of a congregation influences everything from evangelism to opportunities for mission to leadership dynamics. Dr. Rothauge identifies four sizes for American congregations.

- *Family:* 50 worshipers (average Sunday attendance) or less

  This size is aptly named, because the dynamics of these congregations are like those of a family. There is usually a matriarch or patriarch, and the congregation may include one or two actual blood-related families. The priest tends to function as a "chaplain," although there are also new modes of priestly/sacramental leadership through the total ministry modes of pastoral teams functioning in small congregations.

---

6 Arlin J. Rothauge, *Sizing Up a Congregation for New Member Ministry* (New York: Episcopal Church Center, 1982), 193.

- *Pastoral:* 50 to 150 worshipers

  The pastor is truly at the center of the dynamics of this size congregation. He or she is responsible for much of the programming, teaching, and direction. Congregants want to know their pastor and attribute much accountability to that person and role. The pastor is also a primary conduit for welcoming newcomers and for their incorporation into a community.

- *Program:* 150 to 350 worshipers

  Programs dominate the dynamics of the life of this size congregation. People become part of its life through participation in one of these programs or small ministry/fellowship groups. Often there is multiple staff in these churches (especially at the larger end of the grouping). One of the most difficult points of growth in this size is encountered at the point of an average Sunday attendance of about 200.

- *Resource:* more than 350 worshipers

  These congregations are the most complex in terms of organizational dynamics. There are more programs and groups, and often there are subsidiary institutions (schools, foundations, community organizations, and the like). They will usually have many human and financial resources for mission.

Congregational leaders can use this framework as a way of assessing the dynamics of their congregational life. It is absolutely necessary in defining the leadership and program offerings of a congregation and setting expectations about parish life. A great deal of work has been done on the transitional periods a congregation will experience as it moves from one size to another. These periods of transition are fraught with particular challenge and opportunity.

Congregational Life Cycle

Arlin Rothauge has again provided the foundation for these findings through his presentation of the dynamics of congregational life cycle.[7] Using learnings about the human life cycle and studies of organizations, he describes the dimensions of birth, growth, development, stability, decline, and (sometimes) death for congregations.

CONGREGATIONAL LIFE CYCLE

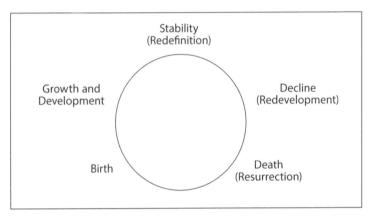

Every congregation is somewhere in its life cycle, as is every living organism. Two things are essential for congregational leaders in their mission direction. First, they must know where they are. When I am working with congregational leaders I invariably have them put an X on the place in the life cycle drawing where they believe they are, so that they can identify and have a conversation about the particular dynamics, challenges, and opportunities which face them at that given point. It is also helpful for leaders to know if they have a common vision about their congregation, or if there is a real difference of viewpoint among them.

---

7   Arlin J. Routhage, "Congregational Life Cycle" (New York: Episcopal Church Center, 2000).

The second thing that leaders must address is their responsibility to shape the future mission of the congregation and approach challenges and opportunities of life cycle in an intentional and planned way. Dr. Rothauge uses three *R*'s to name the interventions offered by leaders: Redefinition, Redevelopment, and Resurrection. At the center of all three is essential reengagement with mission and the development of a vision and plan for congregational development, vitality, and renewal. Different strategies and a different intention are required with these three interventional responses, but mission awareness, articulation, and planning is of the essence to all of them.

Congregational Assessment

The assessment of congregational mission, context, attitudes, and dynamics is essential to everything we have described in this section. There are very useful forms and instruments of assessment currently available to congregational leaders, especially from the Episcopal Church Center, the Alban Institute, and the Gallup Organization. The Episcopal Church Center offers information about average Sunday attendance, membership, and plate and pledge income for every Episcopal congregation and diocese. All clergy and vestries should be aware of this information for their own assessment, and should actually have the ten-year printout available for congregational leaders. In similar fashion, all bishops, standing committees, and diocesan councils should be aware of this information for Episcopal dioceses and their local congregations.

Questions for Your Congregation

1. Are your congregational leaders aware of these frameworks and their importance for understanding a congregation's life and mission?

2. When did your congregation last do an assessment of its context and demographics? What did you learn?

3. How does the size of your congregation affect the way you do your mission and ministry?

4. Where is your congregation in its life cycle?

The Learning Congregation

Learning is one of the primary characteristics of vital and growing congregations. In his book *The Learning Congregation*, Thomas R. Hawkins presents the thesis that learning is *the* appropriate response from and focus of local communities of faith in the time of whitewater change. In response to present challenges, he believes, "We cannot manage our way out of the present crisis with better programs or more sophisticated marketing techniques. Developing a new consciousness of ourselves and our task requires generative learning." He goes on to describe the theological framework for this learning disposition and stance: "Stated theological learning involves conversion . . . . When we learn, we have a fundamental shift of the mind. Learning involves a transformation in our perspective, a change in the mental maps through which we make sense of reality."[8]

A spirit and disposition of education and formation identify the congregation and its life in vital communities of faith. Learning is developed for all ages according to the resources that are available to the congregation. Learning is essential to transformation of individuals and of a congregation. Learning areas include:

---

8 Thomas R. Hawkins, *The Learning Congregation* (Louisville: Westminster John Knox Press, 1997), 20–21.

- *Holy Scripture.* Encountering the narratives that undergird our faith and experience of God can include academic resources, but the type of formation that allows for a more life-based intersection with Scripture is of critical importance.

- *Episcopal identity.* Learning about who we are and the traditions that we share form people in the particular identity of this church, with its hopeful elements of respect, inquiry, openness, and scriptural authenticity.

- *Mission.* Reflection on the present mission of God's church and the opportunities for service and transformation in the world is crucial.

- *Personal call and vocation.* Opportunity should be given to individuals to explore their identity and their call to service and leadership in the church and world.

- *Ministry in daily life.* The congregation should provide the means of learning and reflection on the experiences and meaning of daily living, particularly identifying the points of intersection between faith and daily experience.

- *Context and culture.* Learning about what is really happening in the world around us, with particular attention to issues in our world, context, and culture, is essential.

- *Spiritual practices.* Learning should introduce basic practices that inform and shape Christian life and belief.

- *Marriage, commitment, and family learning.* Congregational learning should offer formation in the areas of human life and relationships that are at the center of the lives that people live day by day.

- *Evangelism.* Teaching people how to tell their own faith stories and to become comfortable in their role of invitation to friends, coworkers, and family is part of learning within the congregation.

There has been substantial progress in the learning and formation experienced by local congregations in recent years. Children, young people, and adults have all benefited from these new efforts and programs that enhance learning and transformation. Some examples include:

- *Godly Play and Catechesis of the Good Shepherd.* Both of these Montessori-based programs have contributed dramatically to the formation of children and their love for and experience of the biblical story. These are hands-on forms of learning where children see and touch biblical images. My own children still recall the power of the *Godly Play* stories they encountered as children in the parish where they grew up.

- *Journey to Adulthood.* This program of catechesis for adolescents has gained wide use and a solid reputation. It is a substantial investment of time in learning—three years—as young people encounter Scripture, story, and learning to assist them in forming their Christian identity. Important rites mark significant transitional moments in the lives of participants. Adult mentoring, service, and pilgrimage are parts of this program of youth transformation.

- *Education for Ministry (EFM) and Disciples of Christ in Community (DOCC).* Both of these programs are for adult learning, using an action/reflection model that joins Scripture and theology with everyday living and experience. They build small communities of learning, fellowship, and leadership that contribute to the transformation of individuals and congregations.

Each of these programs has strengths and weaknesses that make them appropriate for a particular congregation at a particular time. The important thing to remember when discerning which program to choose is that a congregation must set its sights on providing learning and formation opportunities for people of all ages. No single program will fit for everyone, and leaders in the congregation must ensure that there are many opportunities and possibilities for learning. Then formation becomes transformational for children and adults alike.

Questions for Your Congregation

1. Have you done an inventory of Christian formation efforts available in your congregation? What are the strongest offerings? The weakest?
2. How do the children of your congregation find joy in their learning?
3. Are youth and young adults well served in their educational needs?
4. How are adults encouraged to go more deeply into their faith and formation?

A Congregation's Story

The Church of the Holy Communion is a congregation experiencing a real renaissance—a renaissance brought about through learning. It is a growing congregation in a large urban area, a church that not too many years ago had been given up for dead. It was in serious decline to the point of having a total attendance of a couple of dozen people for Easter. Thought had been given to closing the congregation, but its first revitalization came as the parish engaged in committed actions of outreach and service in their local community. There were more people in church but very few children and young people.

That has changed. Holy Communion did its mission reflection and leadership work, engaged its renewing external community more effectively, and learned about the significant amount of new housing that was being built in that community. They decided to invest financial and human resources in learning, education, and formation.

It began with a new look at Christian formation for children. The *Godly Play* formation approach was introduced with great results. Children actually brought their parents to church and to Sunday school, and the number of youngsters in the Christian education program quickly quadrupled. The congregation is now working to introduce *Journey to Adulthood* as a means of formation for their present cadre of youth and for this influx of young children when they arrive at their teenage years.

Adult formation and learning is also a part of the plan for congregational transformation through learning at Holy Communion. A new adult formation working group was commissioned. It had its first meeting and a very interesting conversation. It was discovered that one of the members had completed EFM (Education for Ministry) at another parish and knew that some people at Holy Communion were indicating interest in a group for the parish itself. They decided to work on that, and see where it would go. The good news is that it did go well, and a group now exists in the congregation. The adult formation group has introduced various short-term studies and a long-term centering prayer opportunity for the congregation. Lenten and short-term Bible-study offerings have been well received by the congregation. However, the working group wants to do more. They are now planning two short-term study groups that will be for parents with a focus on parenting and spiritual resources. People seem to be eager for the offering.

Learning is the foundation of the renewal and vitality being experienced in the Church of the Holy Communion. There is the realization that learning is transforming in and of itself. It allows people to explore new areas of their own faith and living. The congregation has also come to realize that focus on children and youth (and now young adults) and their learning is utterly essential to their vitality. The church has opened its doors to a preschool, which is introducing even more children and families to its congregation and its life. Some young parents and other parish members have also joined in a cooperative venture with other congregations to form an "urban" Episcopal School, a school that will serve children who are at risk but who could benefit greatly from this focus of learning.

Learning has translated into vitality for the Church of the Holy Communion. The clergy and lay leaders of the parish have seen people and their congregation transformed by the power of life-long learning. And at Easter last year seven hundred people of all ages showed up.

Evangelism: Plan and Action

"Will you proclaim by word and example the Good News of God in Christ?" That is the question and promise posed about evangelism in the Book of Common Prayer's Baptismal Covenant. The proclamation of Good News is at the very core of Christian mission and congregational life. We are called to present and proclaim God's love through Jesus Christ so that people may be invited into that love.

Episcopalians still remain reticent about evangelism, for a variety of reasons. It is essential that we come to see the urgent call for evangelism in every congregation today. The first reason for that urgency is the gospel itself. The gospel is the good news of hope, peace, joy, strength, fulfillment, and transformation. God wants people to have this news, and those of us who are believers have a particular responsibility for and call to announce this good and joyful news.

The second reason for the urgency of evangelism is the particular moment in which we live. People are searching. They are hungry for meaning in this postmodern world.

There is readiness for the proclamation of the news. But . . . we have not done so well. We are in a systemic decline as a denomination. We are an aging church that has had difficulty in inviting and retaining young people. This is true for our whole denomination, and it is equally true for a majority of our congregations.

What are we to do about this? How do we respond to this urgency as local communities of faith? The answer from the Book of Common Prayer once again: "Proclaim by word and example the Good News of God in Christ." The only way to respond to the urgency is to proclaim the gospel as individuals and as congregations. It is to plan and follow through on actions of invitation and incorporation.

Two basic things are necessary. The first is the willingness and ability of individuals to tell their own faith story and to have the confidence in that story to invite people to consider the message and life of the Christian faith. Individual faith journey stories and reflection provide a foundation for the planning and action of a congregation. Every congregation should have an evangelism committee (whatever the particular nomenclature may be for this important function) and develop a plan for the mission of evangelism. In turn, the vestry has oversight for this important mission action. The *Groundwork* series has provided recommendations for this vestry responsibility.

Particular attention needs to be given to four areas and dynamics of the process of evangelism in the local congregation.

1. Invitation

The first stage of the action of evangelism is invitation. People are invited into the community of faith. There are many modes of invitation. The most important one is personal: people inviting people to the fellowship of faith. Familiarity and internal connection with one's own faith story contribute to the comfort level of believers to invite others to hear the Good News and to become part of the community of faith.

Daily life offers various possibilities for personal invitation. Conversations with other people, especially at times of transition or personal inquiry in the lives of those people, offer special opportunity. The promise of our Baptismal Covenant is to present the Good News "by word and example"; conversations are important, but so are the exemplary actions and witness of service, prayer, and compassion. What are the visible ways that you demonstrate your convictions and beliefs? Personal invitation is the strongest invitation, but there are many other modes of invitation that can be pursued by a congregation.

- *Congregational websites, blogs, and podcasts.* Electronic communication is a newer world for most congregations, but learning how to use it is essential today. An attractive, inviting, and informative website is crucial for every congregation, especially if it wants to invite and attract young adults and youth into its midst. Other modes of electronic communication also offer invitational opportunities.

- *Special event evangelism.* Congregations offer all sorts of special events, such as concerts, lectures, social occasions, even pet blessings. Often they are considered parish events only, even though they are of interest to others outside the local congregation. Intentionally planning and using them for invitation offers a whole new level of evangelism potential.

- *Mailings, door hangers, postcards, and fliers.* Try the simple but effective use of target mailings (lists are available locally) and door hangers. The mailing strategy is more expensive but can be effective, if multiple mailings are used. Door hangers, postcards, and fliers are less expensive and can usually be produced with the talents of parishioners.

- *Community gatherings and service occasions.* Special community events and gatherings are great occasions for invitations. Using some of the other tools described in this section, a congregation can have people and materials of invitation available at everything from the Lions Club fish fry to the charity marathon or walk.

- *Location, location, location.* One of the most invitational possibilities for a congregation is its own setting and location. However, the congregation has to think through how its site and facilities are invitational and how they are not. Signage is an often overlooked possibility.

What can you think of? There are other possibilities for invitation in the life of congregations. What have you thought of? What are you pursuing? What might be done next?

2. Welcome

The second stage of congregational evangelism is welcome. Most congregations of the Episcopal Church identify themselves as warm and welcoming, but what is lacking is the intentional strategy for welcome. Even the best intentions cannot replace plan and action for welcome.

Generally, congregations are more welcoming to people who fit the particular profile of the congregation as it exists in the present. More intentional welcome is required for groups that are not well represented. Attention to the welcome offered to young adults, young families, people whose ethnic identity are not in the norm of a congregation, and others is necessary if a congregation is going to offer real welcome to new groups of people.

The following questions may be helpful as a congregation considers its practice of welcoming newcomers.

- *What do people see?* Is the facility welcoming? Adequate parking, good signage, and quality maintenance are all essential for the "welcoming look." Does the church actually look hopeful in its facilities and "open for business"?

- *How are people greeted?* Or perhaps the question should be, "Are people greeted?" It is not enough to assume that people will feel welcome. Every congregation should have trained greeters who offer a welcome and initial introduction to the worship of the congregation.

- *How are people helped?* Are people left to their own devices, or is there a helpful hand for their first worship or special occasion experience? It is important for visitors and newcomers to have assistance in their Sunday morning experience. People need help with the liturgy and worship. They need to be recognized, welcomed, and accompanied to the social/fellowship part of the occasion.

- *Is there follow-up?* Newcomers and visitors need some kind of follow-up. The research demonstrates that the time elapsed from visit to follow-up makes a difference. The sooner the follow-up, the more likely a visitor is to return. An evangelism plan must include this important dimension.

- *Is initial information about the congregation readily available?* Is there attractive information that describes the congregation and its mission? Does this information invite people to enter the life of the congregation more deeply?

- *Does your congregation effectively welcome people who differ from the "normal" group?* People who are outside the "normal" clientele of a congregation are often invisible—or worse, they are discouraged rather than encouraged to be part of the congregation. Congregational leaders need to be aware of this in reflecting on their congregation's welcome of younger people and others who are not part of the congregation's present characteristic group.

- *Are there welcoming occasions supported by the congregation?* A congregation needs to continue the welcoming process beyond the first experience. Newcomers' groups or events are essential to congregational evangelism. They are helpful occasions for informal and formal welcome.

3. Incorporation

Some congregations leave people at the welcome stage, with members believing that they have completed their evangelism tasks at that point. This is not the case. The real work and experience of transformation occur in the final two stages of the evangelism journey. People need to be invited into their further journey of transformation and into the congregation's life and experience of transformation. How do people enter more deeply into the Christian faith and life? That is the question of the incorporation stage. "Incorporation" means literally "in the body" (from the Latin *in corpus*). This is the point where people enter the Body of Christ in a deep, lasting, and sustained way.

Many traditional Christian spiritual practices are useful for the incorporation process. Similarly, several learning opportunities and programs (Alpha, Via Media, Disciples of Christ in Community, and Education for Ministry) also offer opportunities for going more deeply into Christian belief and practice.

Some learning experiences are focused on people who are entering a congregation or the Christian faith for the first time. Two of them are of particular importance.

- *The Adult Catechumenate.* Based on the Roman Catholic Rites of Christian Initiation, this is intended primarily for adults who express interest in Holy Baptism. It is a program rooted in the practices of the ancient Christian church come alive for people preparing for this sacramental action in our own time.

- *Adult "Journey in Faith" programs.* Many of these programs are based on the catechumenal process but are not focused only on adults preparing for Holy Baptism. Rather, they are learning processes for adults who are examining their own faith and the covenant of their baptism. People for whom the Christian faith is completely a new experience, those who are entering a congregation from some other Christian community or tradition, and longtime church members who want to deepen their faith all benefit from this type of in-depth learning and prayer.

Other learning groups may be used for this incorporation purpose too. The important thing is that the evangelism process points to this deepening experience and intentionally connects people to these programs and opportunities.

4. Sending

The Christian faith is "apostolic" in its very essence, which means that it sends people for mission. The last stage of the evangelism process is sending people into their own ministry, mission, and service. Some people discover their own sense of call in mission. Others require a more focused and intentional structure than is generally available at this time.

It is important for the congregation to find ways of assisting people to discover more about their own sense of call and purpose. Sam Portaro's volume on vocation in this *Transformations* series will assist people in the process of discernment. In addition, four other resources for vocational discernment are of particular use at this time:

- *Listening Hearts.* This personal discernment program helps people to listen to their own hearts and to what God may be saying to them. Its purpose is to help people in decisions and discernment about their own particular call and service.

- *The Gallup "Living Your Strengths" Program.* This assessment book and instrument helps people to discern their particular strengths, styles, and enthusiasms. It makes a direct connection to the type of service and sending that might be most appropriate for individuals.

- Parker Palmer's *A Hidden Wholeness.* This method, rooted in the Quaker tradition, assists people in their vocational search in several ways. One of the most useful is the "clearness committee," a form of communal discernment that helps people to make decisions about their lives, call, opportunities, and potential service.

- Richard Boyatzis and Anne McKee's *Resonant Leadership.* Yes, it's a book on leadership, but it has several tools that can be used by any individual to gain more focus on personal call and service. A congregation can also use other means for the sending stage of the evangelism process. Stewardship programs that emphasize the giving of talent and personal gifts for ministry are effective in the stage. Every congregation should have a clear and up-to-date listing of service ministries that are available through the life of that community of faith.

Questions for Your Congregation

1. Who is responsible for the ministry of evangelism in your own congregation?

2. What are the strengths that your congregation has for inviting, welcoming, incorporating, and sending?

3. What are the barriers to effective evangelism in your congregation?

4. What are the steps you can take to enhance the mission of evangelism?

5. Does your congregation have a plan for evangelism? What actions have been taken to implement the plan? Who is in charge? How is effectiveness evaluated?

A Congregation's Story

The mountainous area around St. Paul's Episcopal Church is lovely, and the town itself is historic and gracious. St. Paul's has been essentially the same size congregation for several generations, blessed with people who love it and the Lord it serves. Both the town and the congregation have long viewed themselves as quintessential small town America, but things are changing.

The town itself is changing rapidly. A new freeway was completed, and the major city that was once three hours away is now accessible in half the time. The result has been a steady development of new housing communities around the town. People are moving in, and both the town and St. Paul's Episcopal Church need to make some response.

The rector and local congregation chose to spend their recent Lenten study to focus on the meaning of and opportunity for evangelism. They had to do some internal work. The congregation has always prided itself on being a "friendly" church full of welcome and warmth. However, they had to be honest that it was easier to do this for each other, as small town folk, rather than for new unknown suburbanites. They considered this and came to a decision: the gospel requires real invitation and the action of evangelism.

They did a "walkabout" of their facilities to see if they were really as welcoming as they purported to be (and even refurbished the parish nursery, horrified to see what they had taken for granted). They developed a door-hanger project, producing a packet of materials and a clear statement of welcome that they delivered to the front doors of the neighborhood. For years they had made the best desserts available at the two town festivals; now they had materials and people available to introduce the church to many newcomers to the community. They offered a pet blessing for the whole town, and it seemed the whole town showed up.

The rector and small evangelism committee have envisioned some further goals for their evangelism efforts. They have trained greeters and created both a "user-friendly" coffee-hour program and a bread-delivery system for newcomers. Now they are working on ways to introduce their church and incorporate the growing number of visitors to their congregation, a congregation that is rapidly growing. It's good news all around.

chapter 5

Suggested Routes
in Stewardship

C. K. Robertson

*It is a shame when the money-raising boys get hold of
so powerful a concept as stewardship and debase it into
a way of increasing church income. Properly taught, the
idea of stewardship can become a means of grace.*

—*The Episcopalian's Dictionary (1974)*

At the heart of this chapter is movement. We are called
to move from an April 15 view of "church taxes" to a
December 25 appreciation of joyful giving. We are called to
move from being predictable to creative. We are called to
move from a once-a-year spotlight on stewardship to a year-
round time frame. We are called to move from a purely financial focus to a more holistic approach, recognizing that it is
not enough to meet the budget. No, the biggest challenge in
moving forward in stewardship is not pledges but people. We

are called to move to a place in our life together where we truly are stewards of all that God has given us, especially one another.

As we engage in this kind of movement, we face several obstacles. To illustrate this, I often ask groups to break up into pairs, with each person sitting back-to-back with his or her partner. One is facing an image of interconnected geometric shapes. That person must then guide their partner to recreate that exact picture, while remaining back-to-back so as not to see the drawer's progress. Likewise, the drawer cannot turn around to see the image and cannot ask questions or respond verbally in any way, just listen, and draw.

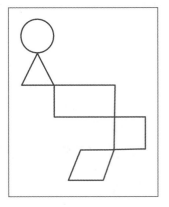

The exercise is timed so that the pair has only sixty seconds, and often I walk about the room during that minute, attempting to distract the various participants while they are in the midst of their task. Once the minute is up, I invite all the various pairs to see how they did. As is probably obvious, there is a lot of laughter at this point, as each pair sees clearly how very difficult the communication of simple shapes really is. How much more the communication of a vision of stewardship! What are some of the obstacles to such communication?

First, there is the time limit itself. In the parish we face similar *time constraints* in the form of deadlines and competing events. School events and extracurricular activities vie with the parish for members' time, and churches do not drop people from the team if they miss a Sunday.

Then there is the obstacle of *one-way communication*. In our exercise, only the person seeing the picture could talk, while the drawer could only listen and draw. This situation may seem contrived, but the fact is that one-way communication abounds in congregations. The greatest example of this is the sermon. Research has clearly shown that simply talking to people is the least effective form of communication, and yet this is exactly what a sermon is. I cannot begin to say how many times I thought I had preached one thing, only to have parishioners make clear to me in their after-service comments that something very different had been heard. Newsletters and bulletins reinforce a sense of unidirectional messaging, and even our websites are often passive and one-way in their format. I am not implying that we should cease preaching or stop sending out newsletters, but it is crucial that we see the potential obstacle to shared meaning that we ourselves set up when we do these things.

There is also the problem of *background noise,* as in the exercise when all the pairs are trying to do their work at the same time. The result is a bit of chaos, as several people are talking at once. Even so, in the parish we may find many people striving to convey a vision of stewardship at the same time, and often without any kind of coordination. The result can be confusing and disconcerting.

And then there is the issue of *language* itself. How often the person speaking assumes that the listener knows exactly what is meant when a word or instruction is conveyed. This can be a deadly assumption. There are, of course, times when it is true. The speaker says to draw a circle and the listener draws a circle. The speaker says to draw a triangle and the listener draws a triangle. But then the speaker says to draw a rhombus (or a parallelogram, or perhaps a weird-shaped diamond thing) and the listener has to figure out whatever that is and is paralyzed in the task or, worse, thinks he/she knows what it is and draws something completely different. I have said many times that Episcopalians speak in tongues far more than most other Christian groups, and we assume that members, not to mention visitors or newcomers, understand what is being said. The classic example of this is the typical Sunday announcements: "The ECW will meet in the narthex immediately following the postlude, while the vestry has a brief meeting scheduled in the nave, and the vergers and altar guild will join the sexton in the sacristy." How we love our Old English language! And when we use other kinds of insider-speak to discuss such important matters as stewardship and giving, we simply add new layers of confusion. As the apostle Paul said in 1 Corinthians 14:19, "I would rather speak five words with my mind, in order to instruct others also, than ten thousand words in a tongue." He goes on to say that it is only the "immature" who use one-way communication or insider language and assume that shared meaning is being experienced. The mature Christian recognizes that talking is not the same as communicating. As James 1:19 says, "Be quick to listen, slow to speak, slow to anger."

Finally, there is the problem posed by *intentional distractions*. A more exotic word for this is "sabotage." In the exercise, I perform this act by going around to the various pairs talking to them about my car, the latest baseball scores, anything that will interrupt the speaker's ability to convey the information about what to draw. How realistic is it to consider that such sabotage is happening in the real world, in our congregations? Only the most naïve church member would not recognize how many times fellow members have sabotaged efforts in stewardship, evangelism, outreach—often doing so unconsciously. Church saboteurs are not necessarily bad or "the enemy," but that does not mean that we can afford to be naïve when it comes to their efforts and the likely disruption to effective communication that results from their actions.

Having considered all these obstacles, then, we can see that a simple ice-breaker exercise with geometric shapes really is not all that different from our real-world situations, as we try to communicate a strong vision of, and strategy for, holistic stewardship. It is imperative that we take into account every possible obstacle and assume nothing . . . except that our assumptions themselves are probably flawed.

Be a Barnabas!

Where, then, does that leave us? Fortunately, we have a scriptural exemplar for what it means to be a model holistic steward in the character of Barnabas (you can read his story in the Book of Acts). Now, it is helpful to explore in practical terms what it might mean for us to "be a Barnabas" in our own time and context, not unlike Francis of Assisi or others in their contexts. To help organize this exploration in a clear, easily remembered manner, the name "Barnabas" itself can be utilized as a mnemonic device, an acronym:

>**B**egin with the big picture
>
>**A**rrange structures strategically
>
>**R**etain and recruit newcomers
>
>**N**urture fellow leaders and stewards
>
>**A**sk for direction and support
>
>**B**udget with vision
>
>**A**nalyze giving patterns
>
>**S**pecify a strategic pledging plan.

Begin with the Big Picture

If we return to the geometric shapes exercise at the start of this chapter, we can say that one of the best ways to help someone else know how to draw the shapes is first to give them the big picture: "It is a series of geometric shapes all joined one to another. First shape, top left is a circle. . . . " For many of our members, stewardship is reduced solely to pledging; it is like focusing solely on the rhombus. We can get caught up in disagreements about that rhombus—about how to approach pledging—without first seeing where it fits within the big picture of a more holistic vision of stewardship, and how it fits with the other pieces that make up that big picture.

This is why, whenever a vestry or group of other congregational leaders ask me to speak with them about stewardship, I do not begin with a presentation of the latest pledge program, but instead ask them a more foundational question: "Why does your church exist?" The response almost always involves either blank stares or something like, "We've been around for over one hundred years!" Their response suggests a misunderstanding of the question. After all, I am not asking *how long* their church has existed, but *why* it exists. This is not a superficial question, and is not unconnected to pledging and similar financial issues. After all, there are other groups that provide for individual and communal needs, and there are certainly wonderful churches of other traditions to which people can choose to belong. What, then, is the point of *this* church? What difference would it make to both the members and the surrounding community if it were not there? And, more to the point, why in the world should I give of my "time, talent, and treasure" to this congregation if I am not clear about its identity and its purpose?

Some church leaders will point out that they have a mission or vision statement. If asked to share it, however, they usually start looking in their vestry manual or church bulletin to find it. They may have worked hard to form that statement, but if they cannot immediately and enthusiastically share it, then I question how real and relevant it is to them. This is why it is crucial to find other ways to discuss identity, vision, and mission. I welcome vision statements and mission statements. I am all too aware, however, that such statements pose the danger of being either too vague to function as a specific marker of a particular congregation (after all, could not every Christian congregation, whatever its denominational affiliation, claim the statement "To know Christ and make Christ known"?), or too lengthy and detailed to be remembered at all (there are many full-page and even two-page mission statements!).

How might we begin to get to the heart of a sense of mission and purpose? One way to begin is to spend some time deliberately reviewing the parish's history. Looking at blocks of three to five years in the church's life, a group may want to ask:

- What was its purpose in that period?
- Who were the leaders, clergy and lay? How did they lead?
- What resistance, if any, did they face? What obstacles were before the church?
- What turning points occurred during this period?
- What significant programs or buildings were created?
- If someone wrote a newspaper article about the church during this period, what would have been the headline? What key points would have been discussed?

Take this information and add to it more detailed oral histories in the form of recorded interviews with longtime members, as well as large givers of record. Why the latter? Simply put, we need to know why our top givers do give. Their remembrances and understandings of the church's identity can help us as we move forward later with the budgeting and pledging phases. We are usually happy to take their money but forget to ask for their input. In many ways, what is being discussed here is something like the first phase of an "Every Member Canvass," only instead of asking for money we are asking for information, which also means we are inviting greater participation and buy-in from our members. What does this have to do with a holistic stewardship program? We are reminding all that where we are going is connected to where we have been before, and that even when we make critical changes in our identity, we can only do so appropriately if we comprehend what it is that we are changing. This is an opportunity to celebrate our past, repent of certain aspects, and as the prophets of old said, *remember*.

While we look back, we can also begin to research the needs of the surrounding community, discovering new possibilities of mission and ministry. This recognizes the fact that we are stewards of our social and physical environment, and the end result is a greater awareness of the impact our church can make in the lives of others. Determine any changing demographics in your vicinity: Which surrounding areas are growing? Who are the people moving there? What kind of materials does the Chamber of Commerce or similar organizations send out? How well known is our church with the Chamber or with realtors, as they are often the first ones to whom people moving into town speak? More than this, approach local agencies and schools to determine their hopes and needs. Churches all too often equate outreach to the most obvious of needs, such as feeding programs or prison ministry. These are wonderful ministries and they need to be done, but outreach can also take the form of new modes of social involvement. For instance, we could buy a block of season tickets to the local high school drama club's plays and advertise in their program, saying something like this: "St. James's Episcopal Church Congratulates the Main Street High Players!" If we do this once, it will be a curiosity; if we make this part of our outreach for at least eighteen months, we will find that this part of the community begins to view us as a church interested in supporting them. We can similarly see if there is a need for a weekly lay-led service at the local nursing home, or find out the needs of the public library.

Host a Series of Parish Events

If possible, it is most advantageous to time the work of discovery and question-asking so that findings are given to the vestry in December, perhaps in time for new vestry members to be on board. This exciting information should then be shared with the whole parish. Such an event may include a potluck dinner with a giant copy of the time line spread across the walls of the parish hall, including key events, clergy, and lay leaders marked in color along the way. The timeline can be drawn in five-year segments on sheets of newsprint or poster board, allowing for easy reading and for space for church members to add to the time line, perhaps putting the year that they came to the parish or adding some important event that is not already listed. In this way, everyone has some part in the creation of the time line.

The Lenten season can be a time of focus on the identity and mission of the congregation through a sharing of stories. Small-group tables are set up in the parish hall at a convenient time each week (Tuesday or Wednesday evenings, for example, or even Sunday mornings between services). Members can be invited to bring with them some kind of tangible token that represents for that person the very essence of the church.

Over several sessions, these items may serve as conversation starters, as parishioners discuss the several common themes that have arisen from the collection of items, themes such as the importance of music for the church, or youth ministry, or hospitality. In other words, a list begins to be created of the key things that make up the essence of the parish at this time in its history. Each session can conclude with Compline from the Prayer Book.

Taking the results of these sessions into the vestry meetings, the church leaders deliberate about one to three new programs or mission foci that can be initiated that year and what it would cost in money, space, time, and human resources to reach the goals. All this can be presented to the parish at Pentecost. Already, the stage has been set for consideration of the budget and pledge campaign for later that year, as well as planned giving, and even a capital campaign if needed.

Before we can even think about choosing a pledge campaign program—focus on the rhombus—we must first outline the big picture and involve as many members as possible in the process of discerning who we are right now and what we believe we are called by God to do together. Once some kind of big picture is formed, it is possible to see how the time, talent, and treasure of the congregation as a whole actually supports or belies their bundle.

Arrange Structures Strategically

A prudent church member once asked me, "I am fully prepared to be a faithful steward, but how do I know that you and the vestry are being good stewards of what you receive from me?" This is a valid question . . . and a good challenge. The clergy and lay leaders are the chief stewards of the parish, and as such, we are called to model the kind of radical holistic stewardship that we ask of our members. It is crucial, then, that we examine all the various structures we set up in the church, and determine if we are being wise and efficient in our use of them. Note that I said *all* the various structures, not just our financial structures. In other words, if a visitor examined our budget, as well as our calendar of events, our list of programs, and our use of human resources (paid and volunteer), what would she or he deduce about our core identity?

One of the best ways to do this is through the use of a mutual ministry review at least once a year to explore how the ordained and lay leaders are spending their time and energy. This is not the same as a typical performance review, which usually is one-sided (the vestry reviewing the rector) and fairly black-and-white (these criteria were met and those were not). Rather, a mutual ministry review supposes that all the leaders are working together to reexamine their priorities and strategies for the sake of the overall mission. For this reason, it is probably most helpful for the review to be somewhat open-ended in its approach. This allows mutual conversation to occur rather than the unidirectional assessment that assumes more of a board of directors and CEO relationship between vestry and rector.

Retain and Recruit Newcomers

One of the most important things I have learned from Barnabas in the Book of Acts is that he saw himself as a steward of newcomers, the Hellenists along with the Hebrew believers in general, and Paul in particular. Successful businesses today will often say that their greatest assets are their customers, but churches all too often forget to take such a view when it comes to the visitors in their midst. To break out of our "insider" tendencies requires intentional efforts.

Create a Newcomer Integration Record

This involves a parish office file of one-page records on every newcomer or new family who comes to the church. The idea here is to follow up on the initial welcome and track people over time, "From First-Time Visitor to Fully Adopted

Member." It is amazing to me how few congregations actually track the kind of information I am describing here, information that is invaluable if we want to bring new members into the parish family. The goal of tracking is not to report on how the newcomer is doing, but on how we as church leaders are doing in following up and responding to the needs of the newcomer.

We are stewards of each person, each individual life that intersects with our common life, and we must take seriously the steps that are needed to bring them along in a way that honors their needs and their gifts. I have been to too many churches where the first thing the visitor receives is a pledge card and an invitation to join the choir. I have seen many others where the leaders are so nervous about possibly scaring someone off that they take a totally passive approach and wait to see if visitors get involved on their own. The Newcomer Integration Record helps parishes find a way between these two extremes that will intentionally, but carefully, increase the odds that a visitor will want to return, get involved, and eventually become an active, pledging member.

Invite Newcomers to Attend an "Invitation-Only" Event

One vital step in the full integration of newcomers is an "invitation-only" event to which they are asked to come. A formal invitation from the vestry is accompanied by a handwritten note from the priest. The event itself is a reception scheduled before the pledge campaign, so that newcomers can learn how the church is organized and spends its money: "We don't want you to be confused when the upcoming pledge campaign occurs. We want you to know how we operate here." Any and all questions are answered. Thus, good stewardship is modeled as newcomers see how their potential pledges of money and time are used.

Initiate a "Membership Moment"

Barnabas understood quite clearly that newcomers to the church are quite possibly the church's greatest assets, and he thereby intentionally reached out in welcome. Perhaps this is why Paul would later instruct the haughty Corinthians that the members of the body need each other and should not imagine it otherwise. A congregation that does not take newcomer incorporation seriously is not taking stewardship seriously.

Nurture Fellow Leaders and Stewards

Barnabas not only welcomed Paul. He also put him to work, nurturing his obvious talents, helping him to be a leader in congregational work. For us, too, newcomer incorporation does not end with the welcoming.

This is why I always ask church leaders, "Are your 'leadership lenses' stuck at 20/80?" We all know the syndrome: 20 percent of the people do 80 percent of the work, and often with some amount of complaining. The repercussions are many, including with pledges. It has been reported that the lowest rate of pledging units comes not from new-comers—who, if asked, will give—but from those who have been in the parish for two years or more but have not been fully incorporated and utilized. This is a no-win game—so the only answer is to change the nature of the game itself. This means stewardship of human resources involves a move toward leadership development, to be a Barnabas who looks for the Pauls around us who need to be nurtured and trained, not simply welcomed. How can this practically be done?

One simple way forward is to consider church events that are currently being held, and think of them as training opportunities for future leaders. For every event, it is crucial that there are co-chairs, one a "veteran" who knows the ways of the church and the other a newer member who can learn the ropes from the more seasoned member. These co-chairs then contact various people in the parish: some long-timers who have not necessarily helped recently, some who simply love to be involved, and some true newcomers, who can be asked to be "buddies." By this term, I mean that these newcomers are asked simply to bring something for a single event. If they respond by saying how new they are, we can explain that we are a church family that does *not* follow a 20/80 principle. Once the event is over, the co-chairs make a point of sending thank-you notes to all those who helped and perhaps calling the newcomer "buddies." In this way, no one person or subgroup becomes responsible for everything that happens, which leads to burnout. Instead, we empower newcomers and help them become "insiders."

This is only one example of intentional nurturing of future leaders. In fact, it really starts when the existing leaders, the clergy and vestry, begin to consider who in the congregation have gifts that are not being utilized at present. This may find its beginning in vestry members praying through their parish directory each month. Even more, it may mean an e-mail going out each week from the church office with the names of any newcomers who filled out a visitor card this week, so that vestry members can pray for those persons in their personal devotions. Imagine the surprised look on a newcomer's face when she introduces herself to a vestry member at coffee hour, and the vestry member says, "Oh, I've been praying for you."

After that, it is crucial for vestry members to move from praying for existing members and newcomers to considering the following possible next steps or even more:

- Think now of who you would like to mentor.

- Consider how you can share what you have learned from your time in leadership.

- Make exit interviews standard procedure for volunteers and staff, as well as for wardens and vestry members.

- Host a "Vocations Fair" where parishioners are invited to have a booth in the parish hall and highlight what they do outside their church work, either in their work or their hobbies.

- Host a series of teaching events that are open to the public, something like "Teaching Tuesdays," on certain themes where your members, including newer members, can draw on their expertise.

One more thing should be said here before moving on. Part of our "church DNA" that we often neglect concerns community involvement. This may be more organically understood in the Church of England, as I learned when I asked a priest to tell me how many parishioners he had. His response startled me: "About twenty thousand people." "What?" I replied incredulously. Realizing the misunderstanding, he responded, "Oh, we have about one hundred thirty members in the church, but the parish is twenty thousand people." I was reminded that the Church of England considers a parish to be the geographical area around the church wherein all the people, unless they claim some other religious affiliation, are to be seen as parishioners for whom the church has responsibility. While there are certainly many problems that can arise from such a "state church" system, as I witnessed firsthand in my years in Britain, I also found that there is much for us to learn from a focus beyond our church walls.

This means helping our members think of their stewardship of time, talent, and treasure beyond the church walls. As one church sign boldly proclaimed:

```
┌─────────────────────────────────────────┐
│   ST.  PAUL'S  EPISCOPAL  CHURCH         │
│      Rector: The Rev. Graham Kincaid     │
│      Ministers: All the members!         │
└─────────────────────────────────────────┘
```

This church has the right idea. A vital part of the work of the leaders of the congregations is to help members understand themselves as fellow ministers and stewards in all aspects of life, not just on Sunday mornings. The church as a whole can choose certain projects that break down the barriers that separate the church from its world.

The key here is for present leaders to make a priority of empowering future leaders. To nurture all the members in their use of time and talent, inside and outside the church walls, is very good stewardship indeed.

Ask for Direction and Support

One day, when I was a rector, I came into the parish office particularly distressed about something; I felt as if the weight of the world was on me. The parish secretary looked at me and said, "Oh, I didn't hear the news." "What news?" I grumbled. "The news that God resigned and you've been named the replacement!" The good news is that God most certainly has not resigned and neither of us have to take God's place. And yet all too often we operate as if we do. The missionary movement in Antioch sent forth Barnabas and Paul only after a time of intentional prayer. Although we are a church marked by "common prayer," the fact remains that all too often we embark on significant projects, stewardship drives, and capital campaigns after having done a lot of preparatory work but without first committing ourselves to prayer, to asking for direction and support from God.

Budget with Vision and
Analyze Giving Patterns

Now we get to the specifics of money. First, before we speak of how to receive money "at the feet of the apostles," we need to consider what giving patterns we have already seen. Earlier, we saw how important it is to make sure that we as church leaders are good and faithful stewards of all that is placed in our hands for the work of mission and ministry. We explored the notion that our essential identity and vision is made real through the various structures of the church, including our facilities, programs, staffing, and budget. We can analyze the pledges and non-pledged contributions of record that have been given in previous years, so that we can better understand and possibly respond to any specific patterns we find. Let's take this step by step and see what we can learn from such an analysis.

The initial categories we want to consider are the more obvious: the numbers of pledging units and the dollars that come from them. It is most helpful to look at this, and the other figures, for at least a five-year period. The longer the period that we can analyze, the better the sense we have of any patterns. Besides pledging units, we also need to include categories for the numbers of NPGs, or non-pledged givers: those who, for whatever reason, don't wish to go on record as pledging but whose own regularity of contributing is equivalent to a pledge. It would be wonderful to see them make a move to pledging, but it is enough for our purposes here that we include them in our analysis. Then, it is interesting to track over time the percentage of pledges that were actually received in the end. In other words, if a total of $200,000 was pledged one year, and yet the actual pledged income received that year was only $180,000, we would say that 90 percent of the total pledged was received.

Having looked at the more obvious figures, we then move into specific areas of change, as we examine both lost and new pledges. First, we consider the number of contributors from the previous year who did not pledge in this year, and the amount of money that was lost because of this decrease. Similarly, we look at the number of new pledges this year and the dollars that came in because of those new pledges. We then consider both increased and decreased pledges from the previous year, and their subsequent dollar amounts. These areas of change are helpful to consider, but to be truly helpful, we should move into even more specific demographics of giving.

Three areas that are of particular interest are age, length of time in the parish, and primary service attended. Age should be no surprise, as we have already considered the importance of understanding generational differences in membership and stewardship. It should be remembered that appeals to "brand loyalty" in order to solicit or raise pledges from younger members of the congregation are, quite simply, futile. At least, this is a working assumption based on understandings of generational differences, but the crucial thing here is to test this assumption by analyzing the giving patterns of members by age groups. Furthermore, it is interesting to see not only how many members in each age category are giving, but also how much they are giving. We may find that there is some real commitment to give in a particular age group, but less ability to give at the same amount as another group—or, again, we may find ourselves surprised by our results. The only way to know is to put the figures down on paper.

Besides age/generation, it is also helpful to consider the length of time members have been attending the church and what effect, if any, that has on their giving patterns. It is largely assumed that the longer a person has been a part of a congregation, the more likely that person is to be a contributor of record and to give more generously. Again, it is important to test that assumption, and see if there are any surprises to be found. It is even more intriguing to cross-reference the age groups with length of time in the church and see if this sparks any "Aha!" moments.

The demographic that focuses on the primary service attended by a giver allows us to explore the differences between the various "congregations within the congregation" that we often have in churches. The expectation here is not parity per se, but awareness of the different patterns.

While our analysis of contributions helps us understand our income, we still need to show our stewardship of financial resources in the way we budget our expenses. We speak of the importance of "pledging units," but "spending units" are equally crucial to the financial stewardship of the parish. Many businesses utilize a zero-based budget, where you start each new fiscal year with a clean sheet and work from there based on the needs of the various departments. This would be a modified version of such a system. The so-called uncontrollable elements would first be examined, including property, utility costs, and staff salaries, asking how the use of facilities and human resources fits with the overall goals of the parish. Then, all the program items can be considered, as the persons responsible for the various areas of mission and ministry show in written form an accounting of what they believe is needed to fulfill those areas.

This next step allows the budget team to make specific recommendations to the leadership that are consistent with the earlier input, beginning from zero and plugging in what is needed or desired. Then the leadership can make the hard decisions that are required of any "tribal elders" and work with the budget team to create a narrative explanation of the proposed budget that shows how every area fits with the overall vision, thereby inviting maximum buy-in from the congregation. As noted above, that budget should reflect a practical version of a vision or mission statement. The budget should be able to "preach well"—the priest's job is to utilize this document in teaching the congregation about their shared mission and ministry. If someone wants to know the vision, the mission, the identity of the church, the budget should be a good indicator.

Specify a Strategic Pledging Plan

Having explored the big picture of identity and vision for the parish, evaluated newcomer incorporation and leadership development, and analyzed parish patterns of financial giving, it is now time to tackle the "rhombus" in that big picture—pledging. As with any of the work already discussed, this step is actually a series of steps or actions, taken over a period of time and starting with the leaders.

Create a Stewardship Statement

Actions speak louder than words, but the first action that needs to be taken involves words: a statement, in fact. I don't mean some vague "spiritual" statement with which anyone can agree but that ends up doing nothing. We all know of pageants where the contestants are asked what they would wish for, only to hear the answer, "World peace!" It sounds good, but there are no specifics, no real commitment to make world peace a reality. A big part of leadership is simply taking the lead. Jesus certainly did this. The apostles and Barnabas and Francis did this. So, too, before we can lay out a strategy for increasing financial giving in the parish, our clergy, lay leaders, staff, commission members, and task force members all need to take the lead by creating an unambiguous stewardship statement that they can sign:

> We, the clergy and lay leaders
> of _____ Church, have
> unanimously and enthusiastically
> committed ourselves to stepping
> up our pledges this year, not
> simply to meet a budget, but to
> help us to go to new levels in our
> ministry and mission. We invite
> our fellow parishioners to join us!

Notice what this actually says. Barnabas gave freely and Paul called on his fellow believers to be "cheerful givers." It is important that our leaders are "unanimous and enthusiastic" in pledging and in choosing to "step up" their pledges. The stepping-up reflects commitment to the big picture that they have endorsed: "We believe in this vision and we are willing to demonstrate that through our increased pledges." The anonymity factor in pledging is not violated here; we do not need to know how much each leader gives or how much they step up that pledge. What is needed is the clear commitment they show individually and as a group to the "new levels in our ministry and mission."

I know this is not easy for some. Making a specific statement of commitment may indeed be a somewhat fearful, threatening task for the leadership, but the fact remains that leaders cannot ask others to do what they will not commit to do themselves. A true turning point for a congregation in terms of their giving comes only when their leaders lead the way. For this reason, the commitment statement, once it is completed and signed, then needs to be posted. The statement should find its way to each congregational leader and group in something of a ratification procedure, recognizing that inasmuch as all of our different leaders really are the chief stewards of a congregation, it all begins with them.

Create an ACTS Commission

Of course, it does not end with the leaders. The clergy and lay leaders should form and publicly bless—appoint and anoint—an ACTS Commission. Why use the name ACTS? This is helpful for a few reasons. First, it takes us out of the dilemma of trying to get people excited to join a "pledge committee," since there is so much baggage that comes with the name. Second, it immediately suggests to people that whatever this is, it is somehow tied into the Acts of the Apostles, a New Testament book full of action and growth and challenges and opportunities. Third, it also ties in directly to the giving program that will be revealed below.

Members of the ACTS Commission receive their marching orders from the vestry or other delegating leaders, tasked with incorporating the detailed analysis and information already gathered into a year-round, personalized, multifaceted giving program. What would such a program look like?

Make It a Year-Round Program

For most congregations October is the church's version of April 15. For this reason, it is important to change the rules of the predictable pledge game by adopting a year-round approach. This does not mean that we suddenly start asking for money all the time, like some stereotypical televangelists, but it does mean utilizing the seasons of the church year to our advantage and making the annual pledge campaign simply one aspect of a larger strategic plan of giving. In that first autumn period, then, the ACTS Commission can do three things.

First, publicize the stewardship statement described above. "This is what your clergy and lay leaders have committed themselves to do. And for what reason? Because they are committed to this vision for the coming year."

Second, the ACTS Commission can offer a fall series of small-group Scripture studies based on the first nine chapters of the book of Acts. A study guide for eight sessions entitled *Acts: From Maintenance to Mission* is available for download free of charge from The Episcopal Network for Stewardship (TENS) website. ACTS Commission members either lead the small groups or train others to do so, and then discuss the results.

Third, the ACTS Commission can announce that it will sponsor several one-time teaching opportunities on money matters at different points in the church year. Utilizing the expertise of parishioners themselves or area experts, the ACTS Commission can offer evening or weekend sessions on specific teachings ranging from tax and investment issues to educating our children in money matters. What this does is to let people know in the church and in the community that the ACTS Commission is committed to helping them become better stewards of all their financial resources, not simply to seeking income for the church. In this way, the ACTS Commission begins to be visible throughout the coming year, and as more than just the fundraising arm of the congregation.

ACTS Dinners

Just as we host an "invitation-only" event for those seeking full inclusion in our extended family, it is helpful to host a subsequent dinner, or multiple "cottage meetings," for everyone in the parish to share in the message that the newcomers receive. Many churches already host events for their members, but they usually use them to talk about how awful the financial situation is and how much they need to meet the budget to save the church. And they rarely host a newcomer event first. Any events that we have need to fit our understanding of the identity and vision, the mission and ministry, of the congregation.

Non-pledging Members

All too often, clergy and lay leaders put a lot of emotional energy into worrying about those members who do not pledge, enough to warrant a few comments here. First, it is important to delineate between those non-pledgers who are in fact givers of record (making regular contributions via check or other identifiable means) and those for whom we have no record of giving at all. Regarding the former, it may be remembered that we marked a special category for "non-pledging givers" in the pledge analysis chart discussed above. It might be useful at some point to approach these persons individually and learn why they choose to give but not pledge. The reasons may vary greatly, from philosophical objections to practical fears. In any case, this is a pastoral task, to be done in a relaxed and safe setting, a task that may yield some positive results both for the parish as a whole and, perhaps most importantly, for the giver—who just might have a story that needs to be shared.

Regarding those who are not on record as giving at all, it might be helpful to review the Newcomer Integration Record on the individuals in question. This might reveal some ways in which we have not followed through in our incorporation of the person along the way. It may also be worth a quiet conversation at some point with the priest, as there may be personal dimensions that can be addressed. However, just as Jesus invited would-be disciples to join him in the journey, *but kept on moving forward whether they joined him or not,* so we must not expend too much energy here, but rather continue to keep the door open to greater participation. Again, this is what pledging is all about: not another financial cause to be supported, but participation in the mission and ministry of God in and through this parish. Pledging is participation! All are called, all are welcome no matter what, but not all may fully participate with their time, talents, and financial resources.

Make It a Multifaceted Program

It is all too easy to focus only on pledges and thereby lose sight of the other avenues of funding ministry for a congregation. This is why it is important for parish leaders to consider the possible need and timing of both a capital campaign and planned giving. There are a number of organizations that can help parishes in these endeavors, most notably the Episcopal Church Foundation, but there are also things that need to be said here about such work.

It has often been said that an annual pledge is "ordinary giving," a capital campaign "extraordinary giving," and a planned gift "ultimate giving." This can be helpful shorthand, but it needs to be unpacked a bit further. The annual pledge is grounded in work of discerning the identity and vision of the congregation.

By giving, we enter into the work of God in and through this parish. If we think of a participation pyramid, that pledge is the foundation, the base of the pyramid. The next level can be considered participation in the health and vitality of the parish in ways that build on the foundation but cannot be accomplished through the base alone. Some other means is required, which is why capital campaign giving is often called "extraordinary," because it literally meets needs that are not possible to meet through the "ordinary" means.

An effective capital campaign follows in its own way many of the steps already discussed. It begins with a discernment of needs on the capital or programmatic level, involving serious exploration on the part of the parish leadership into how certain projects fit and enhance the identity and vision of the congregation. Once the specific needs are clearly determined, along with the corresponding amounts of money required, then a feasibility study is often undertaken. Quite simply, this is the time of securing "buy-in" from parishioners, as participation in the vision is expanded beyond the leadership. As capital campaign expert Glenn Holliman has often said, if this phase is executed correctly—meaning, if the leadership truly incorporates the rest of the congregation in the specified need and cost—then the next phase, the actual asking phase, is not only feasible, but relatively easy. Participation in input leads to participation in income. Any more detailed exploration of a capital campaign process goes beyond these pages. What is relevant here, however, is to recognize that such work is part of the overall stewardship strategy for the parish.

In terms of planned giving, the charge to the parish priest is right in the Book of Common Prayer:

> The Minister of the Congregation is directed to instruct the people, from time to time, about the duty of Christian parents to make prudent provision for the well-being of their families, and of all persons to make wills, while they are in health, arranging for the disposal of their temporal goods, not neglecting, if they are able, to leave bequests for religious and charitable uses. (BCP 445)

There really is no excuse for failing to make planned giving a priority in the parish. Like so much in life, however, this is considered by most clergy and lay leaders to be easier said than done, and usually takes a backseat to the seemingly urgent tasks already before them. What is so sad about the apparent disconnect between intention and reality is that there exists today an unprecedented transfer of wealth in the

United States that will remain untapped by most churches. Those who sacrificed and saved and who put considerable focus on brand loyalty are preparing to make their ultimate gifts to those institutions in which they have invested their heart and soul—and yet churches fail to acknowledge this fact in any visible way. More than this, the wealth they are ready to invest in the future is greater than ever before in history, and yet, again, churches appear unresponsive. When I recently sat down with a member of this "builder" generation and spoke with him about the ultimate gift he could make to the Episcopal Church, he smiled broadly and said, "I have been waiting twenty years for someone to approach me in this way. I love the church, but until now, no one has ever asked me." His words—"no one has ever asked me"—should haunt us in leadership, for when it comes to this kind of ultimate giving, the harvest truly is ripe.

What, then, can we do? The first step is to acknowledge our own nervousness about the issue. Let's face it: we would rather avoid any discussion about money or death. The combination can be particularly intimidating, which is ironic given that we speak of ourselves as a people who believe in resurrection. However, I have found that, our claims each Sunday in the Nicene Creed notwithstanding, most of us in the church live each day as if we believed in immortality, not life after death. It is no kindness to put off important discussions about eternal things with those we love. And for the extended family that is the church to neglect such conversations points to a failure of nerve.

Perhaps I sound overly harsh with all this talk, but it is partly because of my own family circumstance. We always anticipated, because of an age difference and other health issues, that my mother would outlive my father. When she had a massive stroke on Easter morning several years ago, it was a complete shock to our entire family system, and made it clear to me how unprepared I was, indeed all of us were. There were so many things we had not discussed concerning her desires, and Dad's, about so many things. All the questions that would be thrown at us in those initial days following her stroke appeared overwhelming, precisely because we had not thought them through when it would have been much easier and less stressful to do so. At that time I was the rector of a congregation. I immediately decided to change the culture of silence that pervaded my own parish, and help families like mine have access to vital information that they need.

To be faithful stewards of God's gifts, then, means creating a twofold program, both pastoral and practical, for ultimate matters. On the pastoral level, it is helpful to provide a series of educational forums on issues of aging. This can become as much an outreach project to the community as our more traditional understandings of outreach. Topics for the presentations could include the continuum of health care options, from independent living through assisted living centers to nursing care facilities; legal issues surrounding medical decisions, such as a living will and durable power of attorney for health care; financial issues, such as the creation of a last will that reflects your personal values and how to set up power of attorney for financial decision-making; and support possibilities in relation to difficult medical realities like Alzheimer's and other forms of dementia, or home health care. There could be a fifth presentation specifically on funerary issues and final arrangements. For example, most people are unaware that there exist "burial societies" in most states throughout the country that provide a simple burial or cremation for a fraction of the cost charged by most funeral homes.

Throughout the series, by including experts from the community, who may or may not be parishioners, the parish can better connect with the surrounding community, highlighting to these outside organizations that at least one church in the area is serious about the things that are of critical importance—and that we deal with such things as people of both faith and reason. Do not be surprised if you also attract some newcomers to the parish by opening up such a series, and even more if you decide to create or provide space for support groups like those mentioned above.

On the practical level, it is important right now to set up the necessary infrastructure to receive potential planned gifts and also to create a parish file for any "final matters" checklists that are provided for parishioners to utilize and store with the church, as well as in other relevant places (at home, with their adult children, perhaps with their attorney or family physician). Concerning the infrastructure for planned gifts, the Episcopal Church Foundation has created an entire manual entitled *Funding Future Ministry,* which provides sample forms and letters that are necessary for an effective parish endowment structure. There is little sense in duplicating those fine efforts here. What is important is to review some crucial steps.

First, the vestry needs to create the actual fund into which planned gifts would go. This is done by way of a formal resolution, one that includes seemingly obvious but often neglected aspects such as the reason for the fund, the function and formation of a board to help oversee it, and guidelines for when and how the board is to operate. Beyond this, it is also important for policies to be formed regarding the acceptance of gifts. These gifts include simple bequests that are realized after a donor's death, but there are also other possible forms of contribution that can be made during a person's lifetime.

It is, then, important to qualify how the money invested in the fund can be spent and, perhaps even more importantly, how it cannot be spent. The endowment cannot take the place of the ongoing budget, and a planned gift does not supersede an annual pledge.

Again, what is recommended here is a multitiered program of financial giving in the congregation, one that will fund present and future mission and ministry. A capital campaign can hardly be described as successful if it is not built on the foundational piece of healthy annual pledging.

FUNDING PYRAMID

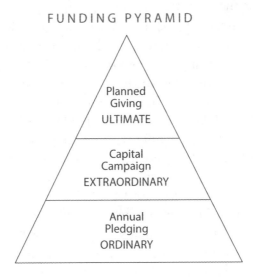

Planned Giving
ULTIMATE

Capital Campaign
EXTRAORDINARY

Annual Pledging
ORDINARY

Don't Forget the Folks Outside

I recall a confirmation service in which the bishop, standing in the entrance to the church immediately before the opening hymn, suddenly turned to face the street outside and made the sign of the cross, nice and bold. Smiling, he turned to me and said, "Always bless the town." It is easy to get so caught up with our internal needs in a parish that we forget the people outside, the community around us of which we are a part. Archbishop William Temple once said that the church is the only institution that exists primarily for the sake of those who are not yet members. God calls us to be stewards not just of one another, but of people outside our church's walls. Like evangelism, outreach is not *apart from* stewardship but *a part of* stewardship. So what does this look like?

OUTREACH PYRAMID

As with the funding pyramid, the key here is to understand that we build on each base. As parishioners embrace opportunities to be stewards of the world around them by addressing the most obvious needs, they can then expand their understanding of outreach by finding ways to reach out to less obvious needs in the community, and then look to more global or environmental concerns as well.

The base of the pyramid consists of the more obvious forms of outreach that we usually think of when we hear the term: feeding the hungry, helping the poor, clothing the naked, visiting those in hospital and prison—in other words, the stuff of Matthew 25. I am speaking, of course, of the parable of the judgment of the nations as "sheep and goats." As followers of Jesus, we all know this parable, and understand in some way that we are called to help "the least of these my brethren." But we also cannot do everything. So, it is important that we as congregational leaders consider two or three projects that we can truly adopt and involve the parish not only financially but also with their time and talents.

Denny and Leesa Bellesi's *The Kingdom Assignment* has been used in several Episcopal congregations to show another way of encouraging the kind of visionary outreach that is being suggested here. Their approach is to give parishioners "seed money" that they then are encouraged to "invest" in some kind of project to make a difference outside themselves. Every time, participants learn that there are opportunities all around them, and in the spirit of St. Francis of Assisi, to discover that "it is in giving that we receive."

It is only after we have helped our parishioners understand the importance of making a difference in the community in obvious ways that we expand our understanding of outreach to include the less obvious. By this, I am referring to the very things that have already been discussed throughout this chapter, namely supporting our local schools, offering "issues of aging" seminars open to the public, and creating support networks that are lacking in our area. If we can adopt a couple of these projects, then we are on our way to becoming a true church for the community.

Relax . . .
and Be Transformed

If all that has been said in this chapter sounds overwhelming at first—"We just want to know how to increase our pledges!"—then take heart that the long-term health and vitality of the congregation and its people more than makes up for the effort involved in what has been outlined. Sure, we can simply do what we have always done, but that is the way of the Church of the Foolish.

Wise ones know that it is crucial to step out of the safety of the boat into the wind and the waves—as long as we keep our eyes on the Savior. The good news for us, as it has been for so many Christians through the centuries, is that we are not God. We can be a little nervous, or even a lot nervous, but let us not hold back from the hard work we have before us because of fear. We are called to be like Barnabas. This means, as we have seen here, that we:

Begin with the big picture

Arrange structures strategically

Retain and recruit newcomers

Nurture fellow leaders and stewards

Ask for direction and support

Budget with vision

Analyze giving patterns

Specify a strategic pledging plan.

Like the gospel parable of the sower and the seed, it is not our job to guarantee the results, only to plant the seed, water it, and watch it grow. Let us dare to leave the results to God. It is not only our methods that need to be transformed, but also our very selves. As so many experts in the field have said, stewardship is about conversion, not budgets and income. When we can allow ourselves to be converted—to be trans-formed—so that we understand that we are stewards of one another, stewards of the newcomers in our midst, stewards of our children and older members, stewards of our community, stewards of our facilities and budget and programs, stewards of the vision that God has given us—then truly we will have become Barnabas!